The Source for Expressive Language Delay

LorRainne Jones

Skill Area:	Expressive Language
Age Level:	2 through 5
Grades:	PreK through K

LinguiSystems

LinguiSystems, Inc.
3100 4th Avenue
East Moline, IL 61244-9700

800-776-4332

Fax: 800-577-4555
E-mail: service@linguisystems.com
Web: linguisystems.com

ISBN 0-7606-0490-8

About the Author

LorRainne Jones, M.A., CCC-SLP, Ph.D., is a speech-language pathologist who has been in private practice since 1989 and is currently with KID-PRO Therapy Services, Inc., in Tampa. This facility includes speech-language pathologists and occupational and physical therapists who treat children with significant sensory-processing deficits as well as severe communication deficits, such as central auditory-processing disorders, developmental delay, and language and learning disabilities. Prior to opening her own practice, LorRainne was a visiting assistant professor in the Child and Family Studies Department of the Florida Mental Health Institute at the University of South Florida in Tampa.

LorRainne currently specializes in treating children with autism or PDD and children who exhibit severely challenging behavior. She has expertise in applied behavior analysis, precision teaching, and interaction-based treatment approaches, such as "floor time."

Before moving to Florida in 1987, LorRainne worked in school programs for children with moderate to severe disabilities in both Michigan and Massachusetts. While in Michigan, she also worked as Special Education Coordinator for Curriculum, Staff Development, and Training for the Northville Public School District, northwest of Detroit.

LorRainne and her husband, Alonzo, have three wonderful children: Allison, Lindsey, and Jared.

The Source for Expressive Language Delay is LorRainne's first publication with LinguiSystems.

Dedication

This book is dedicated to the children—my own children and the children I have treated over the years. My gratitude to each of you is boundless.

Artwork

Cover designed by Mike Paustian

Illustrations by Margaret Warner

Table of Contents

Introduction

Have you ever felt overwhelmed by the severity and variety of problems presented by many children diagnosed with expressive language delay?

Have you ever sensed that language stimulation is just not enough, but felt unsure of what else to do?

Have you ever felt somewhat uneasy when the parent of a child with severe expressive language delay asked you, "Will my child talk?"

Today children with expressive language delay (ELD) are more complex than they were years ago. Then children with delayed language were more likely to have come from a disadvantaged environment or to have had chronic ear infections. The treatment of choice was often "language stimulation activities." For many children with ELD today, language stimulation is simply not enough.

What do we know about children with ELD? Language clinicians have known for a long time that cognitive development impacts language acquisition. Now many clinicians feel there are also other dimensions of the child and his development to consider when providing assessment and treatment. Clinicians are now faced with children with "sensory-processing dysfunction" and "challenging behavior" in addition to language delay. Add to the mix the "social-emotional deficits," and what you often have are confused clinicians with many unanswered questions.

This book is designed to answer as many of these unanswered questions as possible by suggesting a new way to look at children with ELD, a new way to look at assessment, and a new way to look at treatment.

Assessing children with ELD requires examining not only language functioning, both receptive and expressive, but also other dimensions of the child's development, including sensory processing, motor development, and social-emotional development.

Based on the profiles children with ELD present during assessment, they fall into one of three categories—children with Type 1 ELD, Type 2 ELD, or Type 3 ELD. Children with Type 1 ELD have simple language delay. Children with Type 2 ELD have language delay and deficits in other dimensions as well. Children with Type 3 ELD have the greatest language disorder and present the most challenges to clinicians, parents, and educators. These are the children who have severe ELD and other challenges.

This book provides assessment strategies appropriate for each type of ELD. Available assessment instruments are listed, and nonstandardized inventories and checklists are included in this resource. Treatment activities are provided for each stage.

The treatment for ELD outlined in this book is a four-stage process:

Stage 1: Getting to Know You
The SLP establishes rapport with the child to facilitate the child's engagement in effective, interactive treatment.

Stage 2: First Words
The child produces single words, using the principles of *play, pleasure, power,* and *practice.*

Stage 3: Then Sentences
The child sequences words into phrases and simple sentences.

Stage 4: Language Grows Up
The child's language patterns become more sophisticated and complex.

Children with ELD often exhibit challenging behavior. Chapter 8 in this book, "Understanding Challenging Behavior," reminds parents and clinicians that challenging behavior is often a form of communication. Strategies for identifying the communicative intent of behaviors and teaching alternative, more socially-acceptable communication behaviors are included in this chapter.

The final chapter in this book, "Language for a Life and a Lifetime," challenges clinicians to make sure that the language they teach children is the language that will make a dramatic difference in the quality of these children's lives today and in years to come.

Besides being full of ideas and challenges, this book is also about fun. The key to successful therapy for children with ELD is that they find the therapy experience enjoyable and something they will want to do again and again. *The Source for Expressive Language Delay* will help you identify activities that will motivate children to talk as they discover both the pleasure and the power of spoken language—first sounds, then words, then sentences, and so on, and so on.

LorRainne Jones

Chapter 1

Children with ELD: Planes, Cars, and Trains

Expressive language delay (ELD) is a communication disorder characterized by a significant delay in spoken language. It is estimated that 8-12% of preschool children have some form of language impairment.[1] By kindergarten, the incidence is 7.4% (8% boys, 6% girls).[2] Expressive language delay can be *specific* or *non-specific*:

> **Specific expressive language delay** refers to a substantial delay in talking as compared to receptive language (understanding what someone says) and cognitive skills, or intelligence. For example, a child with a standard score of 95 on an IQ test, a standard score of 90 on a measure of receptive language, and a standard score of 60 on a measure of expressive language would have a specific expressive language delay. (Average IQ is a standard score of 85-115.)

> **Non-specific expressive language delay** is a substantial delay in talking that is secondary to a diagnosis of another disorder, such as pervasive developmental disorder (PDD) or Down syndrome. These children are often considered to have a *language impairment*. A special category of children with ELD are children with very little or no speech, often classified as children who are mute, nonverbal, or minimally verbal. They may vocalize or produce sounds, but they have tremendous difficulty learning to talk. Some of these children may even produce intelligible words occasionally, yet they are not able to produce a particular word or words when prompted. A parent of such a child might say, "I heard him say ___ once, but I couldn't get him to say it again."

This book addresses only **oral** language delay, both specific and non-specific, and this disorder will be referred to as *expressive language delay* or *ELD*. This book does not address delays in written language skills.

Expanding Our View of Children with ELD

Children with a diagnosis of ELD are alike in that they have delays in spoken language, yet children with ELD are not a homogeneous group. In fact, in many ways, they can be very different. These differences often give us the most insight about how to provide

---

[1] National Institute on Deafness and Other Communication Disorders. *National Strategic Research Plan for Language and Language Impairments, Balance and Balance Disorders, and Voice and Voice Disorders.* NIT Publication No. 97-3217. Bethesda, MD: 1995.

[2] Tomblin, J. B., Smith, E., and Zhang, X. "Prevalence of Specific Language Impairment in Kindergarten Children." *Journal of Speech, Language, Hearing Research,* Vol. 40, 1997.

treatment and what kind of treatment will be most effective. Child psychiatrist Stanley Greenspan, M.D., and child psychologist Serena Weider, Ph.D., (1998) suggest that an "individual differences" approach to intervention for children with disabilities is preferable to intervention based on a disability label:

> "Current diagnostic categories generally summarize a child's symptoms, but often don't tell us enough about the processes underlying a child's challenges—how the child takes in, processes, and responds to information from the world. These three aspects of biology lie at the heart of a child's ability to think, feel, and inter-act. Children with the same label may be more different than they are alike, and children with different labels may be more similar than they are different in terms of their underlying profiles."

To plan appropriate intervention for children with ELD, we must consider each child's skills and functioning, especially in these areas:

- Auditory and Language Processing
- Sensory Processing
- Motor Planning, Coordination, and Sequencing
- Social-Emotional Development

Auditory and Language Processing

Auditory processing is the ability to perceive and assign meaning to sounds, such as a siren, a doorbell, or thunder. **Language processing** is the ability to perceive and assign meaning to verbal information, such as words, sentences, or stories. Many children with ELD do not process auditory information or language well. They appear to be confused by language. Often these children appear to ignore language except for those words that have significance for them, such as the names of famil-iar, important people and sometimes the names of preferred toys and foods. Early on, they may seem to be hard of hearing because they do not respond to language.

Sensory Processing

Sensory processing refers to the ability to perceive and assign meaning to sensations, the information received from seeing, hearing, touching, tasting, or smelling something. Sensory-processing differences or disorders can have a profound effect on children's learning, behavior, and visual-spatial processing. The box on the next page lists typical sensory-processing problems and the behavioral consequences associated with these difficulties.

Motor Development

Motor planning, coordination, and sequencing are specific aspects of sensorimotor processing. **Motor planning** is the ability to plan and carry out an unfamiliar action, such as fastening a button or hopping on one foot. **Motor coordination**

Sensory-Processing Problems	Behavioral Consequences
Difficulty registering sensation	Poor awareness of sensation
Sensory-modulation deficit	Under- or overreaction to sensory information
Sensory defensiveness	Overreaction to sensory information
Sensory-integrative dysfunction	Impaired bilateral coordination Impaired visual perception Poor visual-motor control Motor-planning difficulties

is the ability to carry out action with smooth, fluid movements. **Motor sequencing** is the ability to carry out sequences of actions, such as brushing teeth.

Visual-spatial processing involves awareness of one's body relative to the space around it, such as judging whether a space is large enough to travel through it. Efficient visual-spatial processing helps us do jigsaw puzzles, dial phone numbers, and fit parts of objects together to make them whole.

Children with motor-planning, coordination, and sequencing problems have difficulty with many activities that normal children engage in, such as manipulating toys appropriately. When most children look at a toy, they automatically have some sense of what to do with it. Lacking the ability to understand how a toy might be moved or used, children with motor-planning, coordination, and sequencing problems may only be able to perform very simple movements with the toy, such as dropping it or throwing it. These children may push a toy around or simply line toys up rather than winding knobs to make them go, pushing levers, or manipulating parts of the toy.

Social-Emotional Development

We often think of speech as merely a complex motor behavior, yet there is a strong link between speech and social-emotional development, an important area of child development. **Social-emotional development** involves learning to relate to other people, including understanding and expressing personal wants, needs, and feelings as well as others' wants, needs, and feelings. Greenspan and Weider (1998) and Locke (1993) suggest that speech development is essentially a function of emotional development. Children communicate by using gestures, sounds, facial expressions, and body language long before they learn to speak. When they begin speaking, they talk about things that have strong emotional associations for them.

Types of Children with ELD: Planes, Cars, and Trains

For all children with ELD, the desired goal or destination is the same: spoken language. How a child gets there, in many ways, depends upon the "vehicle" the child represents.

The "vehicle" is the set of deficits and individual differences that make up each individual child. When it comes to ELD, some children are like planes. Others are like cars. Still others are like trains.

Children with Type 1 ELD: Planes

Children with Type 1 ELD are the children most likely to "take off" in terms of learning to talk once therapy begins. Therapy gets them to the right runway, gets them taxiing, and gets them airborne. Language takes off.

Children with Type 1 ELD may have a specific or a non-specific expressive language delay. They may have no cognitive delays, or they may have mild cognitive deficits.

In general, children with Type 1 ELD do not have significant sensory-processing deficits. Overall, they form attachments with others and relate well to people. Their language comprehension skills may be normal or show mild-to-moderate deficits. Parents of these children often report, "He seems to understand everything I say."

Many children with Type 1 ELD have intact motor-planning skills, but some of them may have motor-planning, coordination, and sequencing as well as visual-spatial processing deficits. The toy manipulation skills of Children with Type 1 ELD vary. These children usually have an extensive gestural repertoire. Although they do not talk, many readily wave bye-bye, blow kisses, tickle, and point. Understandably, some children with Type 1 ELD may exhibit some mild behavioral problems.

Characteristics of Children with Type 1 ELD

- Significantly delayed in learning to talk
- Language-processing skills range from adequate to moderately delayed
- Sensory processing normal or mildly impaired
- Engage or interact with children and adults, but may limit interaction to a few preferred people; considered "shy"
- May have motor-planning, coordination, and sequencing problems
- May have visual-spatial processing deficits
- May have behavior problems due to ineffective communication
- These children often have a separate diagnosis of one of the following:
  - Speech delay (immature speech pronunciation)
  - Developmental delay
  - Down syndrome
  - Mild mental handicap
  - Language delay

Treatment Implications for Children with Type 1 ELD

Intervention is straightforward. With most of these children, traditional language stimulation is often enough to "jump-start" speech. They may be a little shy at first, but with a concerted effort to establish a good rapport, they come around and really enjoy the therapy process.

For some children with Type 1 ELD, general language stimulation is not enough to get expressive language going. Some children with Type 1 ELD respond better to a more direct approach using "prompted imitation" and other direct strategies.

Flying High with Jacob

Jacob was two-and-a-half when I first visited his home to assess his language skills. His mom felt he was quite delayed because he didn't use any words. Instead, he preferred to point. "He's my third child, and he is so different from the girls. By this age, they were speaking in sentences!"

Jacob seemed happy to have a visitor. He was a little shy, but he overcame his shyness once I began pulling toys from my bag. He anxiously moved toward the toys, playing appropriately with each one. As he moved to a different toy, he would look to me to see if it was okay. If Jacob's mom asked him to follow specific commands, he did so without hesitation. Mom was right when she said, "He seems to understand everything I say."

Jacob responded well to a treatment program that emphasized language production during play. His first word was *boom*. *Whee, uh-oh,* and *nite-nite* soon followed. Within nine months, Jacob's talking matched expectations for his age, and he was discharged from therapy.

Children with Type 2 ELD: Cars

Children with Type 2 ELD are the children who take longer to get to their destinations. Planes go as the crow flies; cars can't get there without roads, maps, and lots of direction.

Children with Type 2 ELD have more deficits in most, if not all, areas than children with Type 1 ELD. They have more sensory-processing problems. They are likely to underreact or overreact to sensory stimulation. For many, bonding and attachment beyond the immediate family is more difficult than for other children.

Children with Type 2 ELD often have moderate to severe language and auditory-processing deficits. Some may be echolalic, repeating what they hear other people say. Some may have poor motor planning. Toy play may be limited to a few preferred toys. Sometimes these children are rigid and perseverative in their play. They may have a short attention span and often exhibit challenging behavior.

Characteristics of Children with Type 2 ELD

- Nonverbal or severely delayed in learning to talk

- May be echolalic

- Moderate deficits in receptive language (comprehension)

- May have significant sensory-processing deficits

- May be slow to warm up to strangers—may interact with few people beyond the immediate family

- May have severe deficits in language processing and auditory processing

- Often distractible and impulsive

- May have significant motor-planning, coordination, and sequencing deficits

- May have visual-spatial processing deficits

- May play with only a few preferred toys

- May have challenging behaviors

- These children often have a separate diagnosis of one of the following:

  - Mild to moderate autism or pervasive developmental delay (PDD)

  - Developmental delay with "autistic-like" features

  - Language-learning disability (LLD)

  - Regulatory disorder

  - Multisystem developmental disorder

Treatment Implications

Language stimulation is usually not sufficient to really get these children moving. They often require prompted imitation activities and child-directed, semi-structured learning activities. They also have sensorimotor-processing, motor-planning, and behavioral challenges to consider and address. Treatment presentation style, materials, and activities must be selected carefully to interest and challenge these children without overwhelming them.

On the Road with Amanda

I knew the first time I laid eyes on Amanda that she was going to be a challenge. That mischievous sparkle in her eyes warned me of things to come. Little Amanda was a delightful four-year-old child with Down syndrome.

Interestingly enough, Amanda displayed some behaviors more typically associated with autism. She had difficulty processing sensory information. She was very sensitive to sounds. Her motor planning was poor. Amanda had difficulty manipulating toys, writing utensils, and silverware. She had very little functional communication. She typically echoed the last word or phrase she heard. She often seemed confused by spoken language. She engaged in intense visual examination of toys. Sometimes she moved or flicked items in her peripheral visual field, and her behavior was often a challenge.

Quite by accident, I noticed something interesting about Amanda. For about a two-week period, Amanda, who was typically difficult to manage, was very quiet and more compliant than usual. I also noticed she kept saying "Scary." I did a quick mental inventory. Same building. Same room. Same furniture, same arrangement. I was baffled. What could be scary? A movie? A scary book?

After a few sessions with Amanda's "scary" comments, I remembered that I had added a small container of bubbles to my materials bag. Children with autism are sometimes fearful of bubbles. It dawned on me that maybe Amanda was like these children—afraid of bubbles.

I decided to test my hypothesis. As soon as I reached in my bag and pulled out the bubbles, she yelled, "Scary bubbles, put away!" I quickly removed the bubbles and assured her that I would not bring them back. For the next several sessions, Amanda had to check out the contents of my bag to make sure no bubbles were there. It took several sessions before she was back to her happy, mischievous self, no longer anxious and afraid.

Amanda also had poor motor-planning and sequencing skills. She could not figure out how to manipulate toys or hold a pencil or scissors. When I began working with Amanda, she usually echoed words and phrases. After only a few months of therapy that focused on language processing as well as increasing expressive language skills, Amanda showed a dramatic improvement in using language to express herself. Now, two years later, she speaks in complete sentences and is beginning to read. Her challenging behavior has decreased dramatically. Her motor-planning and sequencing skills are still poor, but improving.

Children with Type 3 ELD: Trains

Children with Type 3 ELD are the children whose every inch along their journeys to spoken language and communication must be engineered. Their journeys may be tedious. Sometimes these journeys are through familiar territory. At other times, the tracks they follow seem to move through areas that few have traveled before.

Children with Type 3 ELD have poor auditory- and language-processing skills. They are often nonverbal. They have severe sensory-processing deficits. They often have severe motor-planning deficits and significant rigidity and perseveration in play. Their interaction and engagement deficits may be severe; significant challenging behaviors occur frequently.

Characteristics of Children with Type 3 ELD

- Nonverbal; may be non-vocal
- May have extremely limited skills for engaging and interacting with others
- May have severe auditory-processing and/or sensory-processing problems
- May engage in self-stimulation
- May perseverate in play
- May have poor motor planning and sequencing
- Often exhibit challenging behavior
- May be very rigid about expected routines

(continued on next page)

Characteristics of Children with Type 3 ELD, *continued*

- These children often have a separate diagnosis of one of the following:

  - Autism

  - Pervasive developmental disorder (PDD)

  - Regulatory disorder

  - Multisystem developmental disorder

Treatment Implications

Children with Type 3 ELD are tough to treat because they are often not interested in play, engagement, interaction, or seemingly anything else. If we are lucky, we can find something that they are interested in, such as foods or toys.

Over time, these children learn that speech has power. They learn that they can get what they want when they say a certain sound or word. They will often imitate sounds to get what they want. Initially, the clinician may be little more than the candy lady or the toy lady—the person who demonstrates what they must say to get what they want and gives it to them. Along the way, these children also learn that communication is fun and that interacting with people can be more interesting and rewarding than food or toys. They learn that communicating with other people is pretty cool.

On Track with Michael

When I first met Michael, he had recently been diagnosed with autism. "Classic autism" was my conclusion after just a few minutes of observing him. Michael was obsessed with car wheels. His mom reported he could push cars back and forth and watch the wheels for hours. He preferred isolation with car wheels and other obsessions. Michael was rigid in his routines and rituals. Some sensitivity to sound was observed, but overall, Michael was hypo-responsive to stimuli in the environment. He craved deep pressure and would often maneuver himself into containers, such as toy boxes—the tighter the squeeze, the better.

(continued on next page)

Michael made only a few sounds. His mom called them "noises." He had been seeing a speech therapist, and his mom was blunt in her assessment. "She played along side him twice a week for three months describing what he was doing. He pretty much ignored her. She was doing the same thing I did for hours a day for over a year, and he ignored me. It hadn't worked for me, and it wasn't working for her, either!"

Mom felt Michael could learn to talk. She knew about sign language and picture symbols, but she wasn't ready for those yet. She felt she couldn't "give up" on speech until someone had really tried to teach him to talk. She thought a different approach might work. She had been doing some reading about the "behavioral approach." Could I help her?

I told her I would do what I called a "child-directed" behavioral approach. I gave her a grossly simplified explanation of how I would teach Michael to talk. First, I would identify the sounds Michael made most frequently. Second, I would identify the foods, toys, and activities he enjoyed most. Third, I would give him a preferred item only when he imitated a sound correctly. After he had a repertoire of sounds he imitated consistently, I would shape successive approximations to get word production and then phrase and sentence production. "But teaching a child to produce speech sounds is only part of the job," I explained. "An equally important part is building an attachment to others—building a basis for communication so that Michael learns to talk because he enjoys the unique, enjoyable, human experience of spoken communication."

Michael's mom was happy with my explanation, and we scheduled his therapy. Michael moved quickly. The three sounds he used to request desired foods soon became words to request everything from candy to tickle games to computer time—words by the hundreds. Phrases and sentences emerged, but more slowly.

Michael is now, as his mom puts it, "spending more time in our world and less in his own little world." He is enrolled in a first-grade classroom with an aide. He is completing Fast ForWord, an Internet-based software

(continued on next page)

program developed by Scientific Learning. The results are promising. He actually responds to a question the first time he hears it, more often than not. He also uses complete sentences much of the time without prompting. He is beginning to read. He completes his worksheets with some assistance. His math skills are emerging.

Michael's social skills are also improving. His favorite thing to do is to play with his two older sisters, an energetic, in-your-face pair—perfect for Michael!

Summary Comments: Same Destination, Different Vehicles

The goal, or destination, for all children with ELD is adequate spoken language skills. Before treatment, these children generally fall into one of three categories:

Children with **Type 1 ELD** generally do well once they are given appropriate language-stimulation activities. Often these activities are enough to get expressive language to "take off."

Children with **Type 2 ELD** have a more severe problem using spoken language to communicate and often need more specific, intense, direct intervention. Therapy must provide more of a road map and street signs for them to reach their destination of adequate listening and talking skills.

Children with **Type 3 ELD** have the most severe language deficits. These children often need a well-engineered track with no distractions to reach the goal or destination of meaningful communication via spoken language.

Chapter 2

Assessment of Children with ELD

Assessment Philosophy

Often when parents and professionals think of assessment, they think in terms of formal testing and the array of impressive information it provides including standard scores, stanines, percentiles, and age equivalencies.[1] Formal testing certainly tells us important information that may be required to determine eligibility for services. For example, does the child have enough of a language delay to receive therapy services? Formal testing may also be required for accountability. Insurance companies and funding agencies want objective measures of progress to determine if therapy should continue. Often, however, it's what the formal measures **don't** tell us that may be crucial to developing the best treatment plan for a child with expressive language delay (ELD).

Why do SLPs depend on tests and developmental checklists?

One reason we speech-language pathologists have come to rely so heavily on standardized measures, developmental scales, and checklists is because, unfortunately, many of us do not have a thorough understanding of child development. We often look at a child and, without a checklist or scale, don't know what we are looking at or for. In our professional training, many of us were taught only to be able to recognize the existence or absence of "milestone behaviors." If we see something that is not on the checklist, we are not sure what it means. We must remember that standard scores, percentiles, and age equivalencies are only part of the picture of any child with ELD.

The Assessment Process

When assessing young children with ELD, it is obvious that we need to determine what they understand and how and what they communicate. We want to know what speech sounds and words they can produce. Additionally, it is important to look at their social development and play skills. Other areas that are important, but often overlooked, include sensory processing and motor development.

Some children with ELD, particularly Type 2 and Type 3 ELD, can be very difficult to assess. *Difficult to assess* means that the SLP must be more creative in assessing development and more creative in getting information than in some other instances.

[1] See the Glossary of Terms, pages 183-184, for definitions of common testing terminology.

Good sources of information include caregiver interview, direct observation, and direct assessment. A discussion of each of these assessment pieces follows.

Parent or Caregiver Interview

One of the most valuable sources of information about a child is the parent. The interview is often the first contact the SLP has with the parent. Each parent is a treatment partner who is an important member of the team.

Each team member brings many things to the table. Parents bring views of their children. Sometimes their views are accurate; sometimes they are not. But all views are valuable, accurate or inaccurate. They tell us a lot about the parents. Other things tell us a lot, too. The terminology parents use when describing their children is significant. The diagnosis they use or don't use is also significant.

The specific diagnosis a child has been given tells me only that the child has a specific diagnosis; it does not tell me about that specific child. The SLP needs to ask a lot of questions to learn about a specific child. Ask what the child likes and dislikes. Ask about eating and sleeping patterns. Ask about siblings. Ask how a child lets the parent know he wants something or doesn't like something. Ask specific questions about which toys he likes and which toys he fears or dislikes. Ask what sounds the child makes and what words, if any, he now produces or has made in the past. Some suggested interview questions are discussed below and listed on the Caregiver Interview Data form, pages 23-24.

1. "Tell me about your child."

This question conveys to a parent that his or her child is indeed a child and not just a diagnosis. It lets the parent know that what he or she has to say is important and valued. It begins to establish the treatment partnership that must exist between the SLP and the parent. It also gives the parent the opportunity to tell you the things that are important for you to know about the child. We can also learn what terminology or diagnoses the parent uses when referring to the child. Remember, your purpose at this stage is getting information and building a partnership.

2. "What does your child like to do?"

While this may seem like a simple question, it is one of the most important questions in the assessment and team-building process. The parent's response to this question should tell us a lot about the child. It probably tells us something about the child's sensory-processing system. It may tell us about his motor development. It may tell us about his cognitive development. It should tell us about his social-emotional development. It may give us information about what to have in the therapy room in order to assess the child. Having the right things in the room where the assessment will take place should facilitate both assessment and establishing a rapport with the child.

Second, it should allow the parent to first focus on the child's abilities rather than any disabilities. It starts the conversation with something positive for the parent to relate about the child. If the parent does not have positive things to say, that too may tell us how the parent is handling the child's dis-ability or how the family is handling the disability.

3. "What does your child dislike?"

The answer to this question gives us information about a child's sensory processing, social-emotional development, fine- and gross-motor skills, and cognitive development. Children with visual-processing problems may not like certain visual stimuli, such as bubbles. Children who overreact to sound may not like toys that produce sound. If a child doesn't like slides or swings, that may indicate some gravitational insecurity, i.e., he is not comfortable unless his feet are on the ground.

4. "Does your child sleep well?"

The answer to this question might tell us something about the child's sensory system. It might also tell us whether we will be dealing with a child who is well rested and how much he may be able to handle the demands of therapy. It might tell us that it is best to schedule treatment in the morning or late in the day after a nap. It also might tell us about our treatment partner, the parent. For example, if we have a child who does not sleep well and is up at all hours of the night, we can assume that the parent is tired. We might have to move more slowly when placing demands on the parent for carryover at home.

5. "Does your child eat well?"

Again, the answer to this question gives us information about the child's sensory system. Children who are picky eaters usually have some other sensory issues as well. This question might also provide information about food allergies. DOCUMENT ALL REPORTED FOOD ALLERGIES. Throughout treatment, continue to ask about food allergies. As the child grows older, more food allergies might be discovered. We also need to look at poor feeding skills and determine if there is an oral-motor problem as well.

6. "How does your child let you know he wants something?"

The answer to this question tells us how the child communicates. Try to help the parent be as specific as possible. You may have to give the parent some examples of the kinds of communication behavior the child might exhibit, including eye gaze, gestures, vocalizations, or facial expression. Try to use "parent think" and "parent talk"—you are more likely to get the kind of information you want if you ask questions in language that generally matches the way the parent thinks and talks.

7. "How does your child let you know he doesn't like something?"

Information about what the child doesn't like is as important as knowing what he likes. It is also important to know how he communicates his likes and dislikes. Refusal or protest communication can be very efficient; it can also be intense and emotional. If the protest behavior escalates into tantrum behavior, ask how long these tantrums last. This information can sometimes tell us a lot about a child's ability to regulate and recover when he is angry or distraught.

8. "What are your child's favorite toys?"

You may have gotten some of this information in the response to question 1 (see page 19), but it is important to get as much detail as possible. A child's toy preferences will tell you a lot about that child. Furthermore, as you try to establish a rapport with the child, it is important for you to be the source of many of the things the child likes.

9. "Are there any popular characters your child likes and plays with?"

The parent's response to this question tells us about the child's likes and dislikes and provides information that parents don't usually provide unless they are asked.

Children with ELD like commercial characters as well as other children do. These characters become the agents for much of the language and play targeted in therapy. They can also facilitate the evaluation process. The presence of those characters make it more likely the child will enjoy the experience and want to return. Also, commercial characters are relatively easy for the child to recognize and perceive as familiar. It's like fast food. We feel comfortable going to a particular fast-food chain anywhere in the world because we know it will be the same as at home. Kids can be that way with commercial characters. Barney is always the same. We know him when we see him. While everything else in the evaluation room may be relatively unknown to the child, Barney is a known and comfortable entity. It's the old *Ah, yes, a familiar face* phenomena. And, if we are honest with ourselves, there are a fair number of us "world travelers" whose American-ized palates soon long for the familiar taste of a Whopper or a Big Mac. When all the new foods, sounds, and smells of a foreign city overwhelm us, just sitting down in a familiar environment with predictable sensations can be very comforting.

10. "Are there any toys he is afraid of?"

Again, knowing what a child dislikes intensely can tell us a lot about the child. The information may tell us something about the child's sensory-processing system.

11. *"What kinds of things does he appear to understand?"*

Get as much information as possible when you ask this question. Try to determine if the child truly understands language or just follows a familiar routine. Sometimes parents assume more language comprehension than the child may actually have. On the other hand, there are parents who underestimate a child's language comprehension, particularly parents of children who have autism. Often those children respond so selectively that it is assumed that they didn't understand a message. Actually, they often don't respond unless something is of very high interest to them. For example, if you tell a child with autism to go find the shoes that he left in the bathroom, he may not respond. If, on the other hand, you tell him to go find the shoes he left in the bathroom so they can go to Burger King, and the child suddenly leaps up and heads for the bathroom, you can safely assume that your primary problem is not comprehension.

Assessment Day

The parent interview should give us enough information to make some decisions about how we are going to be able to assess the child. Before the child arrives for the assessment, set up the evaluation area to include things the child likes. Select appropriate formal test measures, if any, and have them readily available.

Observation

Observations can be done in an office, in the home, or in a preschool. You will be looking for many things. First, during the observation, see how the child interacts with the people and objects in his environment. Next, verify the information that has been provided by the parents and teachers.

The observation may also be the time when the child begins to get acquainted with you. While he is playing with toys or sitting in Mom's lap, you can engage in comfortable, easy-going conversation with the parent or the staff, putting everyone at ease. Come down to the child's level and position yourself on the floor across from the parent and the child. Be relaxed and comfortable and smile. Remember, observing a child during assessment is actually a two-way process. You are checking out the child, and he is, of course, checking you out as well.

> **The Art of Observation**
>
> Many years ago, I watched several episodes of noted pediatrician Dr. Barry Brazelton's syndicated TV show *What Every Baby Knows*. Although I was, at that point, the mother of two, a three-year-old and an infant, I watched in awe as Dr. Brazelton interpreted actions, facial expressions, and other forms of nonverbal communication of infants and the words, actions, and feelings of children of all ages. Dr. Brazelton wisely and gently guided parents, teaching them how to "read" their children. What I learned from him was that children tell us so much about who they are and what they need. We just have to be able to see it.

Caregiver Interview Data

Child _____ Date of Birth _____ Date _____

Interviewer _____ Interviewee _____ Relationship _____

1. "Tell me about your child."

   _____

   _____

   _____

2. "What does your child like to do?"

   _____

   _____

   _____

3. "What does your child dislike?"

   _____

   _____

   _____

4. "Does your child sleep well?"

   _____

   _____

5. "Does your child eat well?" (DOCUMENT ALL FOOD ALLERGIES.)

   _____

   _____

   _____

6. "How does your child let you know he wants something?"

_____

_____

7. "How does your child let you know he doesn't like something?"

_____

_____

8. "What are your child's favorite toys?"

_____

_____

9. "Are there any popular characters your child likes and plays with?"

_____

_____

10. "Are there any toys he is afraid of?"

_____

_____

11. "What kinds of things does he appear to understand?"

_____

_____

Comments _____

_____

_____

Six Areas of Assessment

Following the observation, more structured, formal testing may be conducted. Both the formal observation and formal testing are designed to get information about these six areas of development:

1. Sensory Processing
2. Motor Development
3. Social-Emotional Development—Symbolic Play
4. Auditory and Language Processing
5. Sound Production
6. Expressive Communication

The following section is an overview of these important developmental areas. A list of Common Assessment Instruments can be found on pages 29 and 30. A Checklist of Strengths and Weaknesses to record both observation and direct assessment results can be found on pages 31-33.

1. Sensory Processing

Sensory processing is what a child does as he takes in, organizes, and makes use of sensory information to function and adapt to the environment. Children have unique preferences for activities, toys, and types of interaction, so it's important to tailor any therapy to suit each child's sensory-processing profile. Here are some strengths and weaknesses to look for in this developmental area:

Strengths
- appropriate response time
- makes transitions readily; adapts to changes in routines, tasks, etc.
- age-appropriate attention span
- interested; engages readily
- no unusual reactions to sounds, sights, touch, or movement
- relaxed

Weaknesses
- delayed responses
- has difficulty making transitions

- distractibility
- "shuts down" or resists certain activities
- exaggerated avoidance responses to sounds, sights, touch, or movement
- hypervigilent (highly alert or anxious)

2. Motor Development

Motor development includes the development of fine-motor and gross-motor skills. *Fine motor* is usually associated with control of muscles to do things with the hands and fingers, such as picking up a button. *Gross motor* is associated with control of the bigger muscles used in activities such as sitting, walking, running, climbing, and jumping. Motor development also includes balance, strength, coordination, sequencing, and motor planning (planning a movement before making the movement).

Children with poor motor development may have difficulty manipulating toys to explore them and to problem-solve. They may have difficulty carrying out sequences of movement, such as social games and routines and finger plays. Here are some strengths and weaknesses to look for in this developmental area:

Strengths	Weaknesses
• manipulates novel toys easily	• has difficulty figuring out how to manipulate novel toys
• exhibits age-appropriate coordination	• appears clumsy
• sequences actions, moving easily from one to the next	• has difficulty sequencing actions
• age-appropriate oral-motor strength and coordination	• may have oral-motor strength and coordination problems
• follows commands that include actions or sequences of actions	• may have difficulty following commands that involve motor behavior

3. Social-Emotional Development—Symbolic Play

Social-emotional development involves the ways a child interacts and engages with others. Symbolic, or pretend, play is an important part of social development. At first, a child plays with toys in an exploratory manner. As the child develops, he begins to use toys and props to pretend. Initially, it is very simple action, such as pushing a toy back and forth. Later, symbolic play becomes more complex, and an entire play schema can develop around a single toy. The truck that was interesting to move back and forth is now a vehicle to take a whole family on an exciting trip to the beach or the zoo.

Strong attachment and engagement can be the foundation for pleasurable and fun communication. Children who have a wide range of emotions are often motivated to find ways to communicate those emotions. Symbolic play is also a vehicle for language that expresses problem-solving and higher-order thinking skills. Here are some strengths and weaknesses to look for in this developmental area:

Strengths	Weaknesses
• engages in simple actions with toys	• makes few or no simple pretend actions with toys
• sequences actions with toys	• makes few or no sequenced actions with toys during pretend play
• produces language or vocalizations related to his actions with toys	• no language produced in conjunction with play actions with toys
• simple emotional themes present in play	• no emotional themes present in play
• problem-solving present in play	• no problem-solving present in play

4. Auditory and Language Processing

Auditory processing is how we take in and use auditory information. A child might have normal hearing acuity but not interpret what she hears effectively. **Language processing** is how the brain organizes and makes use of linguistic information. Too often, we assume that because a child's hearing is within normal limits, her auditory systems must be intact. In reality, the child's peripheral auditory system may be working, as is evidenced by good acuity, but what her brain does with the sounds and words she hears might be the source of the child's problems. If a child does not comprehend language, organize it well, and use it comfortably, it can have a significant impact on the child's expressive language development. Here are some strengths and weaknesses to look for in this developmental area:

Strengths	**Weaknesses**
Auditory Processing	
• shows awareness of auditory stimuli	• selective responses to auditory stimuli
• localizes sounds	• localizes only sounds that interest her
• attends to auditory stimuli	• difficulty attending to auditory stimuli, but doesn't appear overly sensitive to sounds
• shows awareness of sound patterns and rhythms	• has little or no sense of sound patterns or rhythm
• able to discriminate sounds and words in the presence of background noise	• has difficulty processing sounds or words in the presence of background noise
Language Processing	
• comprehends words from a variety of word classes	• has limited comprehension of words; may only understand words with high significance, such as *Mom* or labels for a few preferred objects or actions
• demonstrates comprehension of statements and questions	• appears to have little comprehension of statements or questions except those with high personal significance

5. Sound Production

Sound production includes the sounds the child produces. They may be speech sounds or they may be noises. In either case, they may or may not have any significance in communicating with others. It is very important that we know what sounds the child produces independently and what sounds he can imitate. Here are some strengths and weaknesses to look for in this developmental area:

Strengths	**Weaknesses**
• produces a variety of sounds	• has a limited repertoire of sounds
• imitates when prompted	• does not imitate

6. Expressive Communication

Expressive communication involves the way the child expresses ideas and feelings. It includes verbal and nonverbal communication. Here are some strengths and weaknesses to look for in this developmental area:

Strengths	**Weaknesses**

Nonverbal Communication

Strengths	Weaknesses
• positions self within a few feet of you	• positions self as far away as possible
• will orient toward you	• faces away from you
• exhibits occasional gaze checks	• no eye contact or looks at you only when you are not looking
• accepts toys from you; may give you toys for assistance	• may accept toys from you; may initiate play only with toys you haven't offered
• may vocalize a variety of communicative intentions or emotions	• minimal use of vocalization to express intentions or emotions
• may smile/be outgoing or be more cautious, depending on personality type	

Verbal Communication

Strengths	Weaknesses
• uses some words	• produces only a few intelligible words
• uses some word combinations or phrases	• uses few, if any, word combinations or phrases
• uses some sentences	• uses few, if any, sentences

Mistaken Identity

Several years ago while presenting a workshop, I mentioned to the audience how important it is to know the child's sensory profile when planning an assessment. I told them that sometimes, unknowingly, we make assessment more difficult just by having something in a room that is uncomfortable for the child. A young woman in the audience raised her hand, and when I called on her, she said quietly, "That happened to me." I asked her to explain. She went on to relate an experience she had as a very young child.

A teacher had felt she was very bright and suggested testing her for gifted education services. Her mother made an appointment with a psychologist and took her in for the testing. When the child entered the testing room, she noticed an inflated balloon on the shelf. She was so afraid of balloons and the sound they made when they popped that she couldn't concentrate on the testing, fearing the balloon would pop. After the testing, the psychologist informed the mother that her child was not gifted but "retarded" and recommended her for special education. The mother, luckily, decided to get a second opinion and had her child tested again, minus the inflated balloon. The results confirmed that her child was, in fact, gifted!

Common Assessment Instruments

Language and Communication

Bankson Language Test. 2nd Edition. Bankson, N. W. Austin, TX: Pro-Ed, 1990. For children 3-7 years. Yields standard scores and percentile ranks. Three sections: semantic knowledge, morphological syntactic rules, and pragmatics.

Clinical Evaluation of Language Fundamentals—Preschool. Semel, E., Wiig, E., and Secord, W. San Antonio, TX: The Psychological Corporation, 1992. For preschool children. Six subtests: basic concepts, sentence structure, word structure, formulating labels, recalling sentences, and linguistic concepts. Normed.

Communication and Symbolic Behavior Scales. Normed Edition. Wetherby, A. M. and Prizant, B. M. Chicago, IL: Applied Symbolix, 1991. Assesses functional communication in children whose language age is between 9 months and 2 years.

Evaluating Acquired Skills in Communication. Revised Edition. Riley, A. M. San Antonio, TX: The Psychological Corporation, 1984. For children whose skills range from 3 months to 8 years. Assesses three areas: prelanguage, receptive I & II, and expressive I & II. Criterion referenced.

Oral and Written Language Scales. Carrow, Woolfolk, E. Circle Pines, MN: American Guidance Service, 1995, 1996. For ages 3-21 years. Provides standard scores, percentiles, stanines, and test-age equivalencies. Two scales: listening comprehension and oral expression.

Preschool Language Scale-3. Zimmerman, I. L., Steiner, V. G., and Pond, R. E. San Antonio, TX: The Psychological Corporation, 1992. For use with children birth to 6.11 years. Yields standard scores, percentile ranks, and language age equivalency in total language, auditory comprehension, and expressive communication.

Rossetti Infant-Toddler Language Scale. Rossetti, L. East Moline, IL: Linguisystems, 1990. For infants and toddlers birth to 3 years. Assesses six developmental areas: interaction and attachment, gestures, pragmatics, play, language comprehension, and language expression. Criterion referenced.

Sequenced Inventory of Communication Development (SICD). 2nd Edition. Hedrick, D. L., Prather, E. M., and Tobin, A. R. Seattle, WA: University of Washington Press, 1984. For children functioning between 4 months and 4 years of age. Assesses receptive and expressive language.

Common Assessment Instruments, *continued*

Vocabulary

Assessing Semantic Skills Through Everyday Themes (ASSET). Barrett, M., Zachman, L., and Huisingh, R. East Moline, IL: Linguisystems, 1988. For children 3-9 years. Assesses receptive and expressive vocabulary. Ten tasks: understanding labels, identifying categories, identifying attributes, identifying functions, understanding definitions, expressing labels, expressing categories, expressing attributes, expressing functions, and expressing definitions. Normed.

Expressive One-Word Picture Vocabulary Test. Revised Edition. Gardner, M. Circle Pines, MN: American Guidance Service, 1990. For children ages 2.0-11.11. Assesses expressive picture vocabulary. Normed.

Peabody Picture Vocabulary Test. 3rd Edition. Dunn, L. M., and Williams, K. T. Circle Pines, MN: American Guidance Service. For ages 2.5-85+ years. Assesses receptive picture vocabulary. Normed.

Receptive One-Word Picture Vocabulary Test. Gardner, M. Austin, TX: Pro-Ed, 1985. For children 2.0-11.0 years. Assesses receptive picture vocabulary. Normed.

The Expressive Vocabulary Test. Williams, K. T. Circle Pines, MN: American Guidance Service, 1997. For ages 2.5-85+ years. Measures expressive vocabulary and word retrieval. Normed.

Auditory Processing

Goldman Fristoe Woodcock Test of Auditory Discrimination. Goldman, R., Fristoe, M., and Woodcock, C. W. Circle Pines, MN: American Guidance Service, 1970. For children 3 years and older. Subtests: word identification in quiet and word identification in noise. Normed.

Screening Test for Auditory Processing Disorders. San Antonio, TX: The Psychological Corporation, 1986. For children 3-11 years with normal hearing thresholds who have poor listening skills. Three subtests: filtered words, auditory figure-ground, and competing words.

Checklist of Strengths and Weaknesses

Child _____ Date _____ Recorder _____

Check all that apply to this child.

Strengths	Weaknesses

Sensory Processing

Strengths	Weaknesses
❏ appropriate response time	❏ delayed responses
❏ makes transitions readily; adapts to changes in routines, tasks, etc.	❏ has difficulty making transitions
❏ age-appropriate attention span	❏ distractibility
❏ interested; engages readily	❏ "shuts down" or resists certain activities
❏ no unusual reactions to sounds, sights, touch, or movement	❏ exaggerated avoidance responses to sounds, sights, touch, or movement
❏ relaxed	❏ hypervigilent (highly alert or anxious)

Motor Development

Strengths	Weaknesses
❏ manipulates novel toys easily	❏ has difficulty figuring out how to manipulate novel toys
❏ exhibits age-appropriate coordination	❏ appears clumsy
❏ sequences actions, moving easily from one to the next	❏ has difficulty sequencing actions
❏ age-appropriate oral-motor strength and coordination	❏ may have oral-motor strength and coordination problems
❏ follows commands that include actions or sequences of actions	❏ may have difficulty following commands that involve motor behavior

Social-Emotional Development—Symbolic Play

Strengths	Weaknesses
❏ engages in simple actions with toys	❏ makes few/no simple pretend actions with toys
❏ sequences actions with toys	❏ makes few or no sequenced actions with toys during pretend play
❏ produces language or vocalizations related to play actions with toys	❏ no language produced in conjunction with play actions with toys
❏ simple emotional themes present in play	❏ no emotional themes present in play
❏ problem-solving present in play	❏ no problem-solving present in play

(continued on next page)

Strengths | Weaknesses

Auditory and Language Processing

Auditory Processing

Strengths	Weaknesses
❏ shows awareness of auditory stimuli	❏ selective responses to auditory stimuli
❏ localizes sounds	❏ localizes only sounds that interest her
❏ attends to auditory stimuli	❏ difficulty attending to auditory stimuli, but doesn't appear overly sensitive to sounds
❏ shows awareness of sound patterns and rhythms	❏ has little or no sense of sound patterns or rhythm
❏ able to discriminate sounds and words in the presence of background noise	❏ has difficulty processing sounds or words in the presence of background noise

Language Processing

Strengths	Weaknesses
❏ comprehends words from a variety of word classes	❏ has limited comprehension of words; may only understand words with high significance, such as *Mom* or labels for a few preferred objects or actions
❏ demonstrates comprehension of sentences and questions	❏ appears to have little comprehension of statements or questions except those with high personal significance

Sound Production

Strengths	Weaknesses
❏ produces a variety of sounds	❏ has a limited repertoire of sounds
❏ imitates when prompted	❏ does not imitate

Expressive Communication

Nonverbal Communication

Strengths	Weaknesses
❏ positions self within a few feet of you	❏ positions self as far away as possible
❏ will orient toward you	❏ faces away from you
❏ exhibits occasional gaze checks	❏ no eye contact or looks at you only when you are not looking
❏ accepts toys from you; may give you toys for assistance	❏ may accept toys from you; may initiate play only with toys you haven't offered
❏ may vocalize a variety of communicative intentions or emotions	❏ minimal use of vocalization to express intentions or emotions
❏ may smile/be outgoing or be more cautious, depending on personality type	

(continued on next page)

Strengths   Weaknesses

Expressive Communication, *continued*	
Verbal Communication ❑ uses some words ❑ uses some word combinations or phrases ❑ uses some sentences	❑ produces only a few intelligible words ❑ uses few, if any, word combinations or phrases ❑ uses few, if any, sentences

Comments _____

_____

_____

_____

_____

_____

_____

_____

_____

Chapter 3

Treatment Stage 1: Getting to Know You

General Considerations

The primary goal of Treatment Stage 1 for a child with expressive language delay (ELD) is establishing rapport with the child. Why is this attachment and interaction so important? In *The Child's Path to Spoken Language*, John Locke suggests that language acquisition is really part of the bonding and attachment that occurs between parent and child:

> "What motivates the child to pay attention to speech, to respond to it? If the child is shaped by nature to pay attention to 'it', we might ask what is 'it'? To the infant, 'it' . . . is the appearance of familiar faces releasing familiar voices that are modulated by moving mouths in coordination with expressive eyes. In my view, infants do not really set out to learn language. Instead, they study the movements of faces and voices—the observable displays of talkers—and gradually accommodate to and reproduce these behaviors. They do this not because they know about language and understand its importance, but because they have a deep biological need to interact emotionally with the people that love and take care of them."

Treatment Perspectives

The child, the parents, and the clinician each bring a different perspective to the therapy experience. It is important to understand each point of view and the feelings that accompany it.

The Child's Perspective

Children with ELD and their parents often have experienced a lot of failure before the parents seek out a speech-language pathologist. These children feel failure each time they see the disappointment and frustration on their parents' faces after trying to get their children to say sounds and words. Some children get so "turned off" by the whole notion of talking that as soon as they hear "(child's name), say _____," they look away, turn away, or move away. The clinician will have to be creative in order to teach such children that sounds and words are pretty cool things.

The Parents' Perspectives

Some parents who have difficulty coping with a child's delays or lack of interaction stop trying to engage the child. These parents often feel that the child's lack of speech is a personal failure. They feel they have failed because the things that they have done to help the child learn to speak, such as talking, playing together, laughing, tickling, and perhaps even demanding, have not worked, yet these same techniques worked well with their other children.

What is particularly frustrating about a child's lack of speech is that, of all the skills children develop, talking is the most closely linked to the strong bonding and attachment that occurs between parents and their children. As any parent knows, the "love affair" that develops between the infant and its parent is like no other. Speech is one of the key behaviors associated with the intense, emotional, parent-child relationship.

In some instances, parents become angry and sometimes even give up the whole process of trying to get their children to talk, often feeling woefully inadequate. These feelings of failure make it imperative that the therapy experience be successful as soon as possible.

A Clinician-Parent Remembers

I vividly remember that by the time my second child, Lindsey, reached 11 months of age, she had been walking two months and had only said one word, *kittycat*. (She was actually referring to a squirrel, but to her it was a *kittycat,* which was close enough for me.) Not to worry, she would develop more speech soon, I was sure. After all, I was doing all the "right" things to stimulate language. I hoped it was only a matter of time.

I started back to work when Lindsey was 17 months old. At the time, she had four or five words. A few weeks after she started at a wonderful family day care, a preschooler at the day care came up to me with a very concerned look on his face. Without saying it directly, he wanted to acknowledge that, in his eyes, I had failed as a mom and needed help. "My mommy is a speech therapist," he informed me, "and she can help Lindsey learn to talk." I was too stunned to say anything. The ever-observant day-care provider stepped up and handled the situation beautifully. "Lindsey's mommy is a speech therapist, too," she said, "and I'm sure she can help Lindsey learn to talk." I felt like such a failure!

At about 20 months, Lindsey finally began to acquire words. By 24 months, she was acquiring words rapidly. She progressed well after that. As a teenager with her own phone, Lindsey, I assure you, has more than made up for those "quiet" early years!

The Clinician's Perspective

As professionals, we make judgments about outcomes during our first encounters with each child with ELD. We shouldn't, but we do. Children with Type 1 ELD, we assume, will talk because all other areas of their development seem to be more or less on target. We also usually feel reasonably certain that most children with Type 2 ELD will learn to talk. Spoken language for children with Type 3 ELD, however, is often far from certain.

Children with Type 3 ELD present the greatest challenge to us as SLPs. When the parents ask us the question *Will my child learn to talk?*, our honest answer is that we don't know. Our worst fear is that, in spite of our most valiant efforts, the child will not acquire spoken language. We give the child a picture-symbol system or signs or both. We quickly point out to the parents that the child is communicating and that signs and picture symbols may actually help the child acquire spoken language. We often fail to acknowledge what parents are feeling—"I may never hear my child say 'Hi, Mom' or 'I love Daddy.'" In our minds, if a child can communicate, we have succeeded as clinicians, but parents find it painful to accept such limited "success."

For many clinicians, the type of success parents are looking for does not come easily with children with Type 3 ELD. Often SLPs are using techniques they have used successfully with children with Type 1 and Type 2 ELD. For non-imitative children with Type 3 ELD, those techniques alone are, unfortunately, not enough. After trying everything in their repertoire of treatment strategies without success, many SLPs assume that a particular child with Type 3 ELD does not have the capacity to learn spoken language. Perhaps with a few more strategies, clinicians could teach children with Type 3 ELD more successfully.

Treatment Stage 1 for ELD

Treatment Stage 1 can be the most important phase of therapy, and yet the child may never utter a word or make a sound. Stage 1 can last a few minutes or a few weeks. Stage 1 is about getting to know the child on a very personal level. What he likes. What he doesn't like. How he looks and acts when he is excited about something. How he looks and acts when he is bored or uninterested in a toy or an activity.

Stage 1 is also about establishing a rapport with the child. *Establishing rapport* means doing those things with and for a child that are fun and interesting to that child. It means understanding and responding to all forms of the child's communication. In short, it means establishing a relationship.

What does it mean to establish a relationship? Some clinicians feel it means the child should feel elated about the time you spend together. We all have some idea of what it means to build a rapport in a clinical sense. But how do we SLPs know what that is or how it feels to have successfully "established a rapport" with a child? Parents have given me some great descriptions:

"His eyes lit up as soon as he heard your voice."

"I can't tell her she has therapy too early in the day because your name is all I will hear the rest of the day!"

"He knows he goes to therapy after school and makes me come early. He is happy to sit an extra half hour in the waiting room until it's his turn."

"At night when we say prayers, I say 'God bless . . . .' He fills in the names. You have joined his list of favorite people. Your name comes after *Mommy and Daddy* but before *Grandma and Grandpa!*"

Getting to Know Communication Behaviors

Getting to know each child means collecting information about how each one communicates. Children who have ELD usually have some ways to communicate. They certainly let their parents know when they like something and when they don't! They also communicate fear, affection, surprise, and often humor; they just don't use words to do it. For example, they might move close to you (proximity) or turn toward you (orientation) to communicate something. These children might tug on your clothing to get your attention or to seek comfort. We have to figure out what these children communicate about, what they like and don't like, what they feel, and how they let us know it.

Use the Communication Behavior Chart on page 38 to collect information about the child's communication repertoire. Keep the chart handy as you begin treatment so that you can note all communication behaviors you observe. Encourage other adults who interact with the child to keep a similar chart, and share the information across settings to keep everyone informed of the child's progress and preferred ways to communicate. Some of the terms on this chart are defined below:

proximity	The child positions himself appropriately close to you.
orientation	The child faces his body toward you.
gesture	The child directs hand or body movement to you; the child may do it along with you.
eye gaze	The child intersects your gaze briefly or for an extended time.
facial expression	The child shows pleasure, discomfort, or protest in his facial expression, possibly while intersecting your eye gaze.
vocalizes	The child makes sounds or sound combinations to indicate a variety of communication functions (asking for something, getting your attention, etc.).

Communication Behavior Chart

Name ____________________ Date ____________ Recorder ________________

Activity ____

Check any communication behaviors observed during this activity.

Communication Behaviors

Behavior Functions	Proximity	Orientation	Gesture	Eye Gaze	Facial Expression	Vocalizes	Says Words
	Preverbal						**Verbal**
Requesting Objects							
Actions							
Social Game							
Comfort							
Permission							
Calling Attention							
Greeting							
Showing Off							
Refusing							

Comments ____

____

____

____

Room Arrangements to Boost Interaction

Some children with Type 2 ELD and many with Type 3 ELD need some help in staying near us as we try to engage them in interactive activities. Often, if we can position these children in a beanbag chair or a swing, we can get them to slow down long enough to participate in the interesting experiences we have in store for them. An occupational therapist familiar with the child may be able to give you some additional strategies to calm the child and improve her attending.

Remember that getting children slowed down so they can focus on activities means enticing them, not forcing them! We want their engagement and inter-action, not their anger.

Here are some specific ideas about physical arrangements during training to boost the likelihood of successful interaction:

- If possible, arrange the child's training area into centers or play areas within the room, such as a book or reading area, a symbolic-play area, and an area for tabletop activities.

- Some children are more likely to interact while they are sitting in beanbag chairs or in a swing. If you don't have either of these available in the speech area, try to gain access to an occupational therapy area; you'll probably find both swings and beanbags there.

- Arrange for face-to-face interaction as much as possible. Try to keep your face at the same level as the child's. Many parents of very active children use high chairs to "slow the child down" or to get face-to-face with the child.

- While the child is restricted to a high chair, a beanbag chair, a swing, etc., include some motor activities in whatever you present so that the child can still enjoy moving, even if in a limited space.

Sequencing Activities to Boost Interaction

Here are some tips for presenting activities in a sequence most likely to facilitate positive interaction with the child:

- Observe the child briefly as your session starts. Note the child's emotions and interests in various toys or activities.

- Begin the session with play with a toy to allow the child to get "warmed up" and physically acclimated to the therapy environment. Then move to more interactive activities, such as finger plays, social games, and social routines.

- As needed during training, intersperse "down time" when the child doesn't have to engage and can interact with toys without being asked to do or say anything specific.

- End each training session on a "high note." Make sure the child finishes with an activity she enjoys so that she'll want to come back.

Equipment for Treatment Stage 1

The chart on the following page lists examples of suitable toys and interactive games for Treatment Stage 1 for children with ELD.

Enjoyment: What Does It Look Like?

Typically-developing children learn language **in spite of** what we adults do or don't do to encourage it. Children with ELD are more likely to learn language **because of** what we do. If children are to learn, they must first attend, and when they bother to attend, what they see and experience must pay off in a way that makes them **want** to attend and try. When you know the child, you know what optimal attending and engagement look like. You know how he looks when he enjoys something and is wholly engaged in the learning process. You must strive to keep the child in that state for as long as possible. The child who is happy, smiling, engaged, and watching intently for your next move is more likely to learn and remember.

When have you felt yourself totally enthralled with a person—watching and anticipating every word, totally involved in the experience, sitting on the edge of your seat? Who could the object of your attention be but a skilled, talented performer? We know what keeps our attention. Why is it we expect children, especially children with ELD, to be any different? I am convinced that therapists who work with young children should take Acting or Performance Arts 101 as part of their training. They need to learn to use movement, facial expression, and voice to capture the audience: the child with ELD.

Recently, I got a call from a parent asking us to see a child for speech and occupational therapy. The child had been receiving therapy at another facility, but she had been suspended from that therapy practice until "her behavior improved." Our task as therapists is to make therapy interesting enough that the child has few, if any, behavior problems.

Making Intervention Interesting: Creativity and Spontaneity

When working with young children, you have to be creative and very quickly, too. *Being creative* does not mean that you have to have lots of therapy "stuff"—it means you have to use what you have in very innovative ways.

I don't like using a lot of different toys and materials with children for two reasons. First, with many children with ELD, particularly Type 2 and Type 3, introducing new toys may mean having to go through an adjustment period. When many children with Type 2 or Type 3 ELD see new toys, they see sensory-processing and motor-skill challenges. Often language takes a back seat as they adjust to and learn to use, and then enjoy, a new toy. Second, by demonstrating different ways to use the same materials or toys,

Treatment Stage 1
Children's Favorite Toys, Games, Songs, and Finger Plays

Toys

bubbles
wind-up toys
musical toys
a toy house with a slide
containers with toys or objects inside
empty containers for catching toys
Play-Doh
pop-up toys
stuffed animals
toy vehicles
commercial characters, such as Barney or Mickey Mouse

Social Games and Shared-Play Routines

"Peekaboo"
tickling games
silly sounds, such as "Achoo!" or "Pssssst!"
silly facial expressions
silly movement, such as bobbing your head
acknowledging a mistake by saying "Oh, no!"
dropping something and saying "Uh-oh!" or "Oops!"
variations of "Chase"
"Shaky-Five" handshake
"Push Palms Together" (putting your palms against the child's)
"Foot Five" (putting your feet against the child's)

Finger Plays and Songs

For children with Type 1 or Type 2 ELD, ask the parents what
songs their children like. With some children with Type 2 ELD
and most with Type 3, you'll have to work hard to find something
appealing. Here are some to try:

"If You're Happy and You Know It"
"Head, Shoulders, Knees, and Toes"
"The Eensy-Weensy Spider"
"Twinkle, Twinkle, Little Star"
"Row, Row, Row Your Boat"
"The Wheels on the Bus"

we teach problem-solving, creativity and, in some instances, higher-level cognitive skills. Below and on page 43, I have listed many ways to use bubbles or paper in therapy as examples of general creativity with common objects.

Bubble Fun

Blow bubbles.

Blow bubbles into a box.

Blow a bubble under a table or on a chair.

Blow bubbles through a "tunnel."

Blow bubbles over a toy house.

Blow bubbles over a mountain.

Blow big "daddy" bubbles.

Blow tiny "baby" bubbles.

Blow a bubble and catch it.

Pop a bubble on a shoe, a shirt, or pants.

Pop a bubble on an elbow, a knee, a chin, or hair.

Make it "rain" bubbles.

"Barney pop bubble."

"Pooh pop bubble."

"Piglet pop bubble."

"Pop bubble. Wet!"

"Sticky bubbles."

"Wet bubbles."

Paper Fun

paper ball (roll it, throw it, catch it)

paper airplane

paper rain

paper plate

paper dolls (boys and girls)

paper bird

paper face

paper mask

paper hat

paper book

paper tunnel

paper fan

paper flower

paper horn

drawing

Let Me Entertain You

To keep children engaged and excited about the therapy process, you have to be entertaining but not overwhelming. When you first start working with a child, increase your level of animation in stages; watch for signs that the child is okay before adding the next level. I tend to add animation or drama beginning with facial expressions for *happy, sad, surprised, confused,* and so on. Then I add vocal inflection. It is especially important with vocal inflection to look for signs of "too much." Often it's hands held over the ears. Sometimes the child just turns away. I usually add gestures next. Finally, I occasionally add whole-body movement. All the animation pieces together should equal the perfect entertainment for a particular child. He'll keep his eyes on you and anticipate your every move to see what wonders you have in store for him next! The cartoons on pages 44-46 illustrate the suggested progression of adding animation for entertaining therapy.

Adding Animation to Therapy

Facial Expression

(That's great.)

(Oh, no.)

Facial Expression + Voice

Adding Animation to Therapy, *continued*

Facial Expression + Voice + Gesture

Facial Expression + Voice + Gesture + Posture

Facial Expression + Voice + Gesture + Posture + Movement

Entertaining Mary

Mary was what I call a "hodgepodge kid" in terms of diagnosis. She didn't really fit any one diagnosis because she had several possible diagnoses, including autism, central auditory-processing disorder, and Tourette's syndrome.

When I first started working with Mary, she was five years old. Her language development was significantly delayed, and she had been treated using a behavioral approach. Mary was verbal, but extremely echolalic. She taught me a lot about how to animate therapy—and how **not** to.

During my initial session with Mary, we worked in a therapy room in a newly-remodeled wing of a pediatric therapy facility where I did contract work. The therapy room had a light-gray tile floor, white walls, and nothing else except a small, white table with wooden legs and two small chairs. From the moment she walked in the room, Mary had difficulty attending, and she appeared anxious. She kept looking at the walls and floors. What could she be looking at, I wondered. There was nothing there the least bit visually interesting.

I watched curiously for a few minutes. Then I began reaching in my therapy materials bag, pulling things out. She watched intently as I pulled toys and books out of my bag. I felt we were finally getting somewhere. At least she was attending.

I left the toys and materials on the floor behind me in her view, but out of her reach. I hoped she would request to play with something, but she didn't want to play with the toys or the other materials. Rather, every now and then, she glanced at the materials but attended to me and the task I had presented to her earlier. She stopped looking at the walls and floor and glanced behind me every few minutes, but she was calm and able to attend.

(continued on next page)

47

Interesting, I thought. What was happening, I wondered. It occurred to me that perhaps the room did not have enough visual stimulation and Mary needed more to remain calm and focused. Before she arrived for the next therapy session, I decided to drag a large, red mat from the OT-PT area and place it on the floor behind me in the room. Again Mary was much calmer and less anxious. She was still echolalic, but she was at least calm and attentive.

To further test my hypothesis, after a few sessions, I removed all the mats and other visual stimuli. Mary again became distractible and anxious. The next session, the mats were back and she was calm. Then I decided that if "some" visual stimulation was good, more might be better, so I brought in more mats and bolsters. She became anxious and distractible—too many colors and too many shapes. I decided that two flat mats worked the best: one behind me, contiguously in her visual field when she looked at me, and one on the side away from me.

It had taken me a few sessions to determine the right amount and type of visual stimulation for Mary, but that was only the beginning. I had noticed early on that when I added a lot of inflection to my voice, Mary echoed what I said. When I spoke in a monotone, the frequency of her echolalia decreased. I also noticed that Mary became distracted by facial expression and gestures. When I increased my facial expression, she imitated my facial movement. In addition to "echoing" my facial expression, Mary echoed what I said.

Interestingly enough, when I made a special effort to keep my affect flat and my face and head movement free, Mary could attend to what I said and responded appropriately. Her response to my gestures was the same. When I moved my hands, she immediately imitated my hand movements and become echolalic. When I moved my body, such as leaning into her, away from her, or to one side, she imitated my body

(continued on next page)

movement, but she wouldn't respond verbally at all. No echolalia. Nothing. It was almost as though it took such a conscious and intense effort to produce a larger, whole-body movement that she could not attend to the accompanying speech at all.

By four sessions into therapy, I had it figured out. The mats were placed strategically, and I spoke to Mary in a monotone with no inflection, no facial expression, and no gestures or movement. At that point, we were ready to began therapy in earnest. We worked very hard on improving Mary's auditory and verbal processing. As her processing skills improved over the course of the next 18-24 months, I was able to add animation little by little. First, it was a little more facial expression, then more vocal inflection. I added gestures and movement still later. I also added visual stimuli in the room little by little.

Mary has come a long way since then. Now, except when her allergies are bothering her, she readily handles typical conversational exchanges as well as heightened animation with no problem. When I am tired or distracted and my affect flattens or I use a monotone voice, she asks why I'm angry with her. "Mary," I tell her, "I'm not angry." Once assured that I am not angry, she quickly moves on. She reaches for the teen fashion catalog and leafs through the pages to find the picture of the new shade of blue nail polish she plans to ask her mom to buy on their next trip to the store. Mary has come a long way!

Skill: The child watches the adult during toy play.

Description: The child stays within a few feet of the adult and does not try to leave the area. The child may turn toward the adult, give occasional eye contact, and watch the adult, eventually moving toward sustaining good eye contact and observing the adult.

Materials: Visually interesting toys that are easy to manipulate, such as these:

> toy house with attached doors that open and close
> pop-up toys
> wind-up toys
> familiar commercial character figures from Disney, *Sesame Street*, etc.
> bubbles
> toy vehicles
> toys with sound output (wind-up music toys, record players, etc.)

Children with good motor development also like shape sorters and puzzles.

Procedure:

1. Position yourself within a few feet of the child.

2. Place a few toys between yourself and the child.

3. Select a toy and play with it briefly. Pause and wait for the child's reaction.

> **A child uses these behaviors to signal interest:**
>
> watching
>
> reaching for
>
> vocalizing
>
> smiling

4. Follow the child's lead. If the child looks interested, play with the toy again briefly and pause. If the child moves away or looks away, change toys and repeat the procedures.

5. Play again with the toy or toys the child seemed most interested in. Be sure to have two or three of the same type of toy to substitute when the novelty of the first toy wears off.

6. Try to intersect the child's gaze.

7. Match the child's responses, including sounds and words.

8. On the Sound/Word Inventory, page 52, record any sounds or words the child produces.

Tips for Children with Type 2 or Type 3 ELD

- These children have more motor-planning and coordination deficits. Their disinterest may really be uncertainty as to how to manipulate a toy, so use toys that are easy to manipulate. If the child looks interested but does not reach for or attempt to manipulate a toy, try more demonstration. You could also use hand-over-hand assistance.

- Children with sensory-processing problems are not as trusting of new people and environments as other children. They are often in a "high alert" mode. Be alert for their reactions.

- If children have hyperacute responses to sound, they are probably not sure which toys in an array might produce an unpleasant sound. Look for the child's reactions to sound toys as they are brought into the child's visual field.

- If children have tactile defensiveness, they are not sure if you know that. They are anxious whether you will unknowingly place some uncomfortable texture on their hands. Watch for each child's reactions to items with more or different textures when placed in the child's visual field. If the child shows some aversion, remove that item and put it away immediately.

- If children have gravitational insecurity, they are not sure if you will pick them up or position them in some way that will cause them fear or make them uncomfortable. Watch for their reactions to any position changes.

Sound/Word Inventory

Use this form to keep track of the sounds and/or words the child produces, what they mean, and when the child says them. Pay special attention to the sounds or words the child uses during interaction with others, but list other sounds or words as well. This information will be important during Treatment Stage 2 for ELD.

Child _____

Sound/Word Produced	What It Means	When the Child Says It

Treatment Stage 1: Activity 2

Skill: The child interacts during toy play.

Description: The child participates with an adult in activities such as the following:

blowing bubbles
pushing cars
moving figures down a slide or in and out of a house
playing a toy piano
hiding things in containers
opening and closing containers
dropping things in a container

Materials: Toys from Activity 1, pages 50-52, that the child showed the most interest in.

List preferred toys: _____

_____

_____

_____

_____

Procedure:

1. Position yourself facing the child.

2. Initiate activity or play with a preferred toy.

3. Extend the toy to the child with facial expression, gestures, and words to signal "your turn."

4. Pause and give the child time to respond in some way.

5. Match the child's response, and then pause.

6. Signal "your turn" again.

7. Continue for as many exchanges as possible.

8. Note any sound or words produced by the child on the Sound/Word Inventory, page 52.

Tips for Children with Type 2 or Type 3 ELD

Initially, some children with Type 2 or Type 3 ELD may not want to participate. Here are some things to try:

- Give the child a toy that is a little harder to manipulate, and encourage him to ask for assistance by extending the toy toward you.

- If the child likes to line up toys, you put the "next one" in the line.

- If the toy has a door or a chute or the toy is some sort of container, hand the child things one at a time to place inside.

- Some children appear bound and determined to play alone. In these cases, try using friendly "interference." Try to get any kind of interaction, even if it is part of the child's effort to avoid interacting constructively with you. For example, if the child is pushing a car, drive your car in front of his. He then has to acknowledge your interference by moving around your car.

- Some children will interact only if you have something they want. Get a toy similar to the one the child is enjoying. Begin to play with it, and then encourage the child to trade toys.

Treatment Stage 1: Activity 3

Skill: The child participates in social games, social routines, songs, and finger plays.

Description: The child responds to social games, social routines, songs and/or finger plays, sustaining the interaction for several exchanges.

Materials: none

Procedure:

1. Present an action or a phrase from a social game, a song, or a finger play.

2. Pause before saying the last word of the phrase. Wait expectantly, and then signal the child that you expect a response.

3. When the child produces some sort of response—sound, gesture, or movement—say the desired response to give the child a model.

4. Continue for several exchanges.

5. If the child does not respond or seem interested in the particular finger play, song, or game presented, go on to another one.

6. Note any sounds or words produced by the child on the Sound/Word Inventory, page 52.

Throughout this activity, entice the child to interact with you. Here are some specific ways to make yourself the most interesting toy in the room:

- Make your motions interesting. Sometimes exaggerated movement helps.

- Play with your voice as well. Sometimes whispering gets children's attention. Emphasize certain words by saying them louder or more slowly. Vary your pitch. Make silly sounds.

- Make your facial expressions interesting. Smile and make silly faces. Laugh or pretend to cry.

- Remember to watch the child's reaction to each variation as you add interest to an activity.

Tips for Children with Type 2 or Type 3 ELD

- These children are more difficult to engage. You may have to make the games, songs, or finger plays even more exaggerated in sound, movement, and facial expression.

- Sometimes games with a good deal of sensory input are more likely to engage children. An eensy-weensy spider that "crawls" firmly up the child's arms or legs may be just the extra boost the child needs to anticipate and sustain interaction.

- Children who prefer proprioceptive input often like push and pull games. Push against each other's hands. Release and push again. Also try singing and acting out "Row, Row, Row Your Boat."

- Sometimes variations on "High Five" get a child interacting. "Shaky Five" is a favorite: as you extend a hand for "High Five," take the child's hand and hold it firmly. Shake it back and forth as you say "Shaaaaaaaky five!"

- Sometimes I can get a child involved by "hiding" a toy figure in a sock. After she takes that toy out, I hide another one in her other sock—then a pocket and maybe a shirt sleeve. Be sure to make it fun. At first, the child is caught off guard by the game. Usually she comes around after a few exchanges. If not, try something else. Be creative. Don't give up!

Chapter 4

Treatment Stage 2: First Words for Types 1 and 2 ELD

The Principles of Play, Pleasure, Power, and Practice

Truly effective and comprehensive treatment for children with Type 1 or Type 2 expressive language delay (ELD) must incorporate the principles of **play**, **pleasure**, **power**, and **practice**.

The Play Principle (Therapy in Disguise!)

Why disguise therapy?

> Two speech-language pathologists walk into a therapy office waiting room. They approach you, a three-year-old child with ELD.
>
> One says, "Let's go. Time for speech therapy."
>
> The other one says, "Let's go. Time to play!"
>
> Think about it. Which SLP would you go with?

Play is a "kid" thing. Most children with Type 1 or Type 2 ELD know on some level that play is fun, and they know they feel good when they play. When I see young children in therapy, I never use the words *therapy, work, learn,* or *learn to talk*. When children go with me, they know it is time to *play. Play* is a familiar concept for children. It has a very positive connotation.

Participate in therapy is more difficult to understand and, therefore, tends to be viewed with some apprehension. It is an unknown entity to siblings and typical playmates. When asked to come into *therapy* with a child, they may feel uncertain and uneasy because *therapy* is a serious, adult word. The same children, though, are eager to come along and *play*.

The child must be interested in the play activities in order for the treatment to be successful. To foster the child's engagement and attachment, the clinician or parent must be willing to interact creatively and spontaneously with the child on the child's level, using play with a surgeon's precision to accomplish specific therapeutic goals. To the casual observer and the child, good therapy looks like play, yet it is really precision therapy in which an adult is simultaneously addressing many goals that will develop and refine the skills that will eventually lead to the child's competency in cognitive, emotional, and communication development.

> Good play is precise therapy.
> Enjoy the process!

I have met with some skepticism early in the therapy process when I have asked parents to do carryover activities at home that involve play. They look at me with concern when I say, "I want you to play with your child." Often, they feel they should be doing more. After all, they reason, they have already been playing with their children, and so far it hasn't worked—the children aren't talking. I explain that they must learn to play with their children in a different way.

Additionally, emphasizing play allows parents opportunities to enjoy and have fun with their children. Often parents focus so much on their children's disabilities and deficits, they cannot comfortably do something as "mundane" and "trivial" as play with their special-needs child when there are so many significant problems.

> **When parents and professionals put themselves in a play mode, they encourage the creativity and spontaneity necessary to keep young children enamored with the therapy experience and not just "attending to task." There is a difference!**

Parents need to view play differently—to allow themselves to engage in activities that are fun. This change in perspective is extremely important. Parents of children with disabilities can and should feel the joy of their children's pleasure without feeling guilty about it.

The Pleasure Principle

Some children enjoy producing words solely because they are fun to say. These are my *Whee, Boom,* and *Uh-oh* kids. These are the children who won't say "Eat" or "Ball" or much of anything else when prompted. But many of these same children, when presented with a very interesting word combined with action and drama to go with it, suddenly find speech something worth doing. They put Barney on a slide and push him down, saying "Whee!" Or there is the child who thinks it's pretty cool to push a car off a table and say "Boom." There is also the child who loves to look at the picture of Barney sleeping and say "Shhhhhhhh."

Children are interested in producing language that has strong emotional content for them. Not only does producing it make them feel good emotionally, in a lot of instances, these early fun words feel good from a sensorimotor standpoint and are fun to produce. They sound cool, too!

As children acquire basic language skills, they learn that language is powerful—they learn to use language to control behavior. As a first step, though, speaking is a "feel good" phenomena for young children.

The Power Principle

Some children with ELD are interested in the power of language right from the start. They learn according to the power and pleasure principles. Many children don't respond to parents' efforts to get them to speak readily or respond to such requests in the therapy setting. Why? The parents know and respond to the children's nonverbal communication. These children often realize that the SLP, on the other hand, doesn't know them and doesn't know what they want. If a child wants something and Mom isn't there to bail him out, then he may have to request it in a more conventional manner. He may think that it will be hard and that the SLP will prompt for something he can't say, but the SLP will prompt for sounds or words with the highest likelihood of success.

Some children with significant sensory-processing deficits, severe autism, or pervasive developmental disorder (PDD) are not interested in interacting with others or find it too difficult to process emotional and physical sensations and language all at the same time. Play as a therapeutic strategy may overwhelm these youngsters.

Many of these children learn early speech according to the **power principle**. They will produce speech to get something. These are the kids who use language to ask for something and to refuse to do something. They respond to contingent reinforcement: "If you want X, then you have to say Y." These children often benefit from behavioral intervention and discrete trial training early on. We must also teach them the pleasure principle, however, as soon as possible.

The Practice Principle

Regardless of which motivates a child to acquire speech early on, pleasure or power, the **practice principle** holds true. The more often a child produces target sounds, sound combinations, words, word combinations, and so forth, the better he gets at it. Remember that speech production is, at its most basic level, innervation of particular parts of the brain in a particular pattern. Also, speaking is like any other skill—the more you practice it, the better you get at it.

Given the value of practice, the issue of frequency of production becomes important. We must target a higher production number for speech targets if we want to increase the rate of speech acquisition. Too often in speech therapy, we rely on general play, and in a single 30-minute speech session, a child may produce target sounds or words only a few times. If you are learning a new skill and you only practice it infrequently, you will not become proficient. Throughout activities for Treatment Stage 2, try to elicit as many repetitions of words from the child as possible to maximize the child's opportunities to practice new words.

Early Vocabulary Words

Children's early vocabulary words can be grouped into three general categories—pleasure words, pleasure and power words, and power words. (Some of these "words" are actually two words that function together as one word to the child, such as *go potty*.)

Pleasure words are strongly appealing to children. They are generally words that have an intense sensorimotor component and, therefore, an intense emotional component. The words themselves may be fun to say, and they may have an interesting sensory experience to go along with them, such as *pop* or *quack*.

Pleasure and power words are fun to say or have value as concepts that may not have strong sensorimotor and/or emotional content loading for a child, such as *between* or *smooth*.

Power words are functional words or phrases that have low or average sensorimotor or emotional loading for the child, such as *ankle* or *same*. Children only use these terms because of their linguistic and communication features.

To illustrate the differences among these three categories of words, let's look at three action words: *tickle, eat,* and *point*.

Tickle is fun to hear and to say. It is associated with an activity that has strong sensorimotor features and a strong emotional association. *Tickle* is a **pleasure** word.

Eat has strong sensory loading but also has a strong functional component because it is necessary for survival. It can have positive and negative emotional loading. For young children, *eat* is a **pleasure and power** word.

Being tickled and eating are incredibly intense, whole-body experiences. When you are tickled and you enjoy it, it is wonderful; if you don't enjoy it, it can be almost painful. Eating can be pleasurable or not so pleasurable. Before a child eats, he may get very hungry and may become tense, uncomfortable, and less likely to tolerate frustration and demands. After the child eats, his system is usually more balanced and better able to handle the demands of the environment.

Point is a very functional concept, but it has very little sensorimotor or emotional loading. The mere act of pointing gives very little back to the child. For young children, *point* is a **power** word.

Pages 61-69 list common vocabulary concepts for children ranging in age from early preschool to later elementary school. The words are grouped into categories and sorted into **pleasure**, **pleasure and power**, and **power** terms. Keep in mind that each child is unique; what serves as a "pleasure word" for one child might function as a "power word" for another child. A word that is extremely relevant to one child might be irrelevant to another. We have to figure out each child's pleasure, pleasure and power, and power words based on the child's skills, interest, and frequent contexts.

Early Vocabulary Words

Pleasure	Pleasure and Power	Power
Actions		
hop	eat	make
push	sit	put on
pull	stand	point
tickle	drink	touch
blow	hide	go potty
march	scare	cut
take off	draw	color
clap	wave	study
wash	whisper	drive
pop	pat	
run	see	
slide (whee)	hear	
swing (whee)	brush	
go	hit	
cry	yell	
splash	lie (down)	
fall	skip	
knock, knock		
Toys		
ball	play dough	puzzle
bubbles	book	blocks
balloon	airplane	
squeak toy	shape sorter	
car	teddy bear	
truck	puppet	
choo choo	stack toy	
music	tricycle	
jack-in-the-box	house	
pop-up toy	baby doll	
	telephone	

Early Vocabulary Words, *continued*

Pleasure	Pleasure and Power	Power
Body Parts		
tummy	eyes	arms
fingers	ears	legs
toes	teeth	elbows
hair	knees	chin
nose	chin	eyebrows
		neck
		ankle
		wrist
		eyelashes
Clothing		
hat	shirt	pants
shoes	zipper	dress
socks	sweater	jacket
sneakers	sandals	sleeve
boots	underwear	collar
pajamas	overalls	tie
	button	belt
	shorts	
People		
mama	mechanic	baker
dada	mail carrier	banker
grandpa	farmer	garbage collector
grandma	soldier	jeweler
baby	nurse	plumber
pilot	baseball player	repair person
cowboy	football player	librarian
doctor	waiter	
truck driver	cashier	
bus driver	dentist	
magician	painter	
firefighter	taxi driver	
	carpenter	
	conductor	
	musician	
	coach	

Early Vocabulary Words, *continued*

Pleasure	Pleasure and Power	Power
Descriptors-Quality		
wet	hot	clean
icky	cold	hard
heavy	fast	full
dirty	dark	slow
dark	happy	noisy
	soft	same
	big	different
	quiet	
	loud	
	light	
	rough	
	smooth	
	warm	
	sad	
Descriptors-Quantity		
empty	more	every
full	less	each
long	all	several
one	none	
two	tall	
three	short	
four	wide	
five	narrow	
	most	
	least	
	many	
	few	
	whole	
	half	

Early Vocabulary Words, *continued*

Pleasure	Pleasure and Power	Power
Time Concepts		
now	yesterday	later
soon	tomorrow	never
morning	afternoon	week
night	before	month
first	after	year
	start	hour
	finish	minute
	beginning	second
	end	
	always	
	last	
	day	
	late	
	early	
Position		
in	on	beside
under	in back	next to
off	top	together
up	out of	in front
down	through	apart
around	bottom	ahead of
high	backward	next
low	forward	last
	above	right
	between	left
	inside	corner
	outside	near
	middle	far

Early Vocabulary Words, *continued*

Pleasure	Pleasure and Power	Power
Places		
playroom	McDonald's	hospital
home	grocery store	doctor's office
pool	drugstore	church
playground	school	dry cleaners
mall	fire station	
toy store	gym	
ice cream store	car wash	
movies		

Pleasure	Pleasure and Power	Power
Animals/Animal Sounds		
meow	cat	crab
ruff	dog	seal
moo	chick	raccoon
ssss	snake	goat
quack	duck	goose
neigh	horse	rhinoceros
roar	bear	fox
squeak	shark	eagle
ribbit	ladybug	beaver
oink	ant	wolf
baa, baa	lion	
buzz	tiger	
peep, peep	butterfly	
	mouse	
	squirrel	
	bird	
	fish	
	dinosaur	
	snail	
	owl	
	caterpillar	
	deer	
	worm	
	octopus	
	zebra	
	hippopotamus	
	whale	

Early Vocabulary Words, *continued*

Pleasure	Pleasure and Power	Power
Transportation		
choo choo	train	submarine
car	truck	
bus	helicopter	
beep beep	bike	
vroom	tractor	
plane	spaceship	
	jet	
	jeep	
	golf cart	
	van	
Tools		
hammer	nails	
screwdriver	screw	
wrench	paint	
drill	ladder	
paintbrush	lawn mower	
	shovel	
	hose	
	rake	
Characters		
Barney		
Baby Bop		
Pooh		
Piglet		
Eeyore		
Tigger		
Mickey		
Minnie		
Big Bird		
Cookie Monster		
Elmo		
Bert		
Ernie		
Po		
Dipsy		
Tinky Winky		
Laa-Laa		

Early Vocabulary Words, *continued*

Pleasure	Pleasure and Power	Power
Food		
cookie	milk	tea
juice	ice cream	coffee
candy	peanut butter	mustard
French fries	banana	ketchup
pop	apple	beans
hot dog	orange	pears
Coke/pop/soda	waffle	salt
cracker	pancakes	pepper
Popsicle	bacon	
hamburger	sandwich	
chicken fingers	jelly	
pizza	grapes	
	carrots	
	butter	
	potatoes	
	cake	
	soup	
	pie	
	eggs	
	water	
Self Care		
thermometer	vitamins	deodorant
makeup	cologne	prescription
exercise	shaving cream	scales
	hair dryer	
	Band-Aid	
Recreation/Leisure		
park	baseball	tennis
slide	basketball	soccer
swing	football	jogging
hopscotch	boat(ing)	oar (rowing)
skating	bowling	volleyball
seesaw	gymnastics	sailing

Early Vocabulary Words, *continued*

Pleasure	Pleasure and Power	Power
Household Objects		
VCR	tape	
TV	box	film
camera	bag	stove
pillow	clock	refrigerator
computer	cup	napkin
light	spoon	glass
fish bowl	towel	fork
	sink	container
	bottle	jar
	soap	can opener
	mop	washing machine
	bucket	dryer
	broom	microwave oven
	birdcage	drawer
	basket	counter
	vacuum	light bulb
	dishwasher	plastic
	plate	metal
	mixer	paper
	toaster	cloth
	fan	
House-Inside		
bedroom	kitchen	basement
family room	bathroom	upstairs
porch	living room	downstairs
	dining room	ceiling
	closet	walls
	window	carpet
	blinds	tile
	steps	back door
	curtains	front door
House-Outside		
roof	driveway	
chimney	fence	
garage	tree	
flowers	grass	
pool	bushes	

Early Vocabulary Words, *continued*

Pleasure	Pleasure and Power	Power
School		
paper	tape	chalkboard
scissors	desk	ruler
marker	cubby	calculator
glue	backpack	compass
crayons	chalk	bathroom
paint	pencil	cafeteria
gym	pen	exit
	media center	fire drill
	auditorium	
	lunch box	
Colors/Shapes		
circle	orange	gray
dot	yellow	tan
line	blue	octagon
	green	
	purple	
	pink	
	white	
	brown	
	black	
	square	
	triangle	
	rectangle	
	oval	
	diamond	
	cross	
Nature/Science		
sunny	plant	leaf
rainy	seeds	stem
cloudy	flower	petal
windy	dirt	branches
snowy	tree	trunk
icy	lake	river
beach		valley
		waterfall

Treatment Stage 2 (Types 1 and 2 ELD): Activity 1

Skill: The child produces words during play and social interaction.

Description: The child produces first words in the context of social play and/or toy play.

Materials: Preferred toys (Review your list from page 53.)

Procedure: 1. Position yourself facing the child.

       2. Present a word from the First Words—Pleasure list (pages 71-72), accompanied with an appropriate movement or gesture.

       3. Wait expectantly for a response. If the child does not produce the target word, repeat steps 1 and 2 a few more times. If the child still doesn't produce the target word, select another word from the list and repeat the procedure.

       4. When the child produces the target sound, repeat it back to her.

       5. Continue with the same target word for as long as possible, but change materials to maintain the child's interest. For example, if you are putting toy figures down a slide and saying "whee," you could switch to a toy house with a chute and slide figures down the chute.

       6. Switch to a new word from the First Words—Pleasure list. Try to get the child to say each target word as many times as possible.

Tip for Children with Type 2 or Type 3 ELD

If a child does not imitate and doesn't respond to prompts, it may be necessary to teach her to imitate sounds and words more directly. Chapter 5, pages 76-93, covers how to teach speech production to a child who doesn't imitate.

First Words—Pleasure

Pleasure Words	Activities to Elicit These Words
Whee	Move toy figures down a slide and say "Whee!" Move a toy figure on a toy merry-go-round and say "Whee!"
Uh-oh	Say "Uh-oh!" as you make toy figures fall off or out of structures. Use appropriate gestures and facial expression, too. Say "Uh-oh!" as you make toys or objects roll off a table. "Accidentally" tip over a basket of toys.
Shhhh	Put several toy characters to bed one at a time. Say "Shhhh" to each one. Put your index finger up to your lips as a gesture. (You can use baby dolls, but they are usually too big to fit multiple figures in a bed and get multiple productions. Remember the practice principle!)
Nite-nite	Put several toy characters to bed one at a time. Say "Shhhh" to each one, putting your index finger up to your lips as a gesture. Pretend to kiss each character, adding voicing to the kiss for emphasis; then say "Nite-nite" to each one. You could also put a cover over the figures as you say "Nite-nite."
Boom	As toy characters slide down the slide, say "Boom!" when each one reaches the bottom. Say "Boom!" as you make vehicles crash into a structure. Say "Boom!" as the child sits down on a beanbag chair.
Knock, knock, knock	Knock on the door of a toy house, a door of the room you're in, or pictures of doors in books.
March, march, march	Say "March, march, march" as you march around the room. Say "March, march, march" as you march toy characters around.
Mmmm	Say "Mmmm" as you pretend to eat toy food. Say "Mmmm" when you read picture books that show eating.
Tickle, tickle, tickle	Play a tickle game. Tell the child that you are going to tickle her and tell her where on her body you are going to tickle her. Match your tickling movement to the rhythm of your words as you say "Tickle, tickle, tickle."

First Words—Pleasure, *continued*

Pleasure Words	Activities to Elicit These Words
Pop, pop, pop	For this bubble activity, use a regular bubble wand, and position it close to your face to encourage eye contact. Never blow directly into the child's face. Make sure the child is aware that you are about to begin blowing. As you pop bubbles, say "Pop, pop, pop!"
Push	Use toys with buttons to push. As you push a button, say "Push!" Say "Push!" as the child pushes on a scooter board or as you push the child on a swing.
Whoa	While sitting on the floor, pretend to lose your balance. Say "Whoa!" as you rock to one side and then the other side. Match the timing of "Whoa!" to your movement to each side.
Achoo	Pretend to sneeze. Exaggerate your sound, your body movement, and your facial expression.
Wow	Use a kaleidoscope. Say "Wow!" to comment on the great view.
Boo	Play "Peekaboo." As you pop into view, say "Peeka-___" and signal the child to fill in "boo." Be sure to use "Peekaboo" gestures. Make sure your sounds match your actions.
Animal sounds	As you play with toy animals, make appropriate animal sounds. Match your sounds to your movement of each animal, and exaggerate the sounds to add interest. Here are some example sounds for various animals:

Animal	Sound
bee	buzz
dog	ruff, ruff
cow	moo
duck	quack, quack, quack
bird	peep, peep, peep
cat	meow
snake	sssss
lion	roar

Skill:　　　　　The child produces words to regulate others' behavior.

Description:　　The child produces first words to request desired items, activities, or people, and says "No" to indicate refusal.

Materials:　　　Preferred toys, foods, and activities
A few items the child probably won't be interested in

Procedure:

1. Observe the child. Determine what is of interest to the child that day.

2. Make sure the item the child desires is out of reach. Play dumb when the child reaches or gestures to get the item.

3. Select an appropriate activity and target word from First Words—Power, page 74. Prompt the child to say the target word.

4. Repeat the word back to the child as you give him the desired item. Really emphasize the word by saying it several times as the child is engaged with the item.

5. You could also give the child choices of preferred items and items the child probably doesn't want. Prompt the child to say the name of each item he wants. You could also prompt the child to say "No" to refuse an item he doesn't want.

Tip for Children with Type 2 or Type 3 ELD

Children with Type 2 or Type 3 ELD who have poor attending and imitation skills may require specialized strategies using "shaping" or reinforcement of successive approximations. Please refer to Chapter 5, pages 76-93, for specific shaping techniques.

First Words—Power

Power Words	Activities to Elicit These Words
No	Give the child something you know she doesn't want, and prompt the child to say "No."
All done	Continue an activity when you know the child is ready to move on. Prompt for *All done* with question inflection, gesture, and facial expression. Wait for the child's response.
Bye-bye	Say and wave "Bye-bye" at the end of a session. You could say "Bye-bye" to the toys as you put them away.
Eat	When the child is hungry, offer a choice of playing with a toy or eating *(Eat)*.
Juice, water, cookie, crackers, chip	Offer the child choices of foods and beverages. Position the items just out of the child's reach so that the child has to ask for specific items. Pretend not to understand the child's gestures or eye communication; wait for the child to say something.
Book, ball, bubbles	Place the toys out of the child's reach. Pretend you don't know which toy the child wants. To prompt the child, say the name of each of the choices.
That	Again place an item out of reach. Prompt for *That* with a pointing gesture as you say "That."
Up, down	Have something the child cannot see unless she is picked up to see it. Say "Up" to prompt the child. Play a gesture game with the child. Hold the child's hands. Move the child's arms as you model "Up" and "Down" and "Up" and "Down." Exaggerate the movement and your word productions.
Open	Have transparent containers with little toys inside. Prompt the child to say "Open."
On, off	Use toys with on-off switches. Prompt the child to say "On" and "Off" during play.
Pull, push	Use toys that can be pushed or pulled. For example, use a scooter board and prompt the child to say "Push" and "Pull."

Treatment Stage 2 (Types 1 and 2 ELD): Activity 3

Skill: The child's vocabulary expands.

Description: The child begins to acquire new words, including nouns, action words, describing words, location words, and pronouns.

Materials: Select appropriate toys for the play theme, such as any of these:

toy foods	toy furniture
toy animals	toy house
toy tools	books
toy vehicles	play dough
clothing	puzzles
family/character figures	baby doll and bed
toy stove	

Procedure: 1. Select a familiar play theme, such as a birthday party.

2. Select one or two sets of toys, such as food and characters.

3. Incorporate simple actions with the toys as you enact the drama of the play theme.

4. Prompt the child to imitate target words. Target only a few new words each session.

5. Prompt the child to produce the target words independently.

6. Intersperse previous target words with the new target words so that the child experiences success and maintains old vocabulary words.

Tip for Children with Type 2 or Type 3 ELD

If a child doesn't imitate and doesn't respond to prompts, it may be necessary to teach her to imitate words more directly. Chapter 5, pages 76-93, covers how to teach speech production to a child who doesn't imitate.

Chapter 5

Treatment Stage 2: First Words for Type 3 ELD

Not Pleasure, Not Power: Then What?

Some children, usually those with Type 3 expressive language delay (ELD), have difficulty imitating others. Speech-language pathologists working with these children often select an augmentative communication system as the primary means of communication, such as sign language or a communication board. This type of communication system usually includes continued, but diminished, focus on speech-sound production.

Once forced to introduce an alternative communication system, many parents and professionals make assumptions about long-term outcomes. These assumptions typically include lower expectations for language and cognitive development; these children are not expected to acquire functional speech communication.

Rather than assume these children may not acquire spoken language, it might be the time to use a very highly-specialized method of treatment in which we precisely "shape" speech production. This shaping is accomplished through reinforcement of successive approximations, using the principles of applied behavior analysis (ABA).

Shaping is an important strategy in ABA-based instructional programs, which are often referred to as "precision teaching." In most university settings, those who are taught the principles of precision teaching are in programs for behavioral psychologists and/or certified behavior analysts. Unfortunately, those who are trained in the principles of ABA instruction often apply the principles in a rigid, adult-directed approach. With children who have Type 3 ELD, such instruction can and should be modified to become child-directed. It should be based very much on play and interaction. We can make precision teaching "child friendly" and, to some extent, child directed as we reinforce successive approximations. That way, we systematically move a child from producing sounds and noises to producing functional speech and later to producing sophisticated speech communication that fully supports cognitive and emotional development.

This chapter has two sections, Getting Ready (pages 77-85) and Treatment Activities (pages 86-93). Getting Ready outlines information to gather and decisions to make before starting effective treatment. Treatment Activities lists specific target skills and explains how to teach them.

Getting Ready

The Sound Inventory: "What He Can Say"

During the initial evaluation and the first few sessions with the child, note any and all vocalizations on the Sound/Word Inventory, page 52. Also note the activity the child is involved in when producing the sound. You should also have a list of the child's sounds provided by the parent prior to the evaluation. Be sure to ask the parent to note any and all new sounds the child begins to produce at home once treatment begins. Ask the parent to note what the sounds were, during which activities they were produced, and with whom.

Use the questions below to help complete and analyze the Sound/Word Inventory.

What types of sound productions are on the list?

It is important to identify a child's complete sound repertoire. If there are very few consonants and a lot of vowels, that tells us that acquiring intelligible speech may be more difficult because there is a whole class of sounds the child is not producing. Limited consonants may suggest that a motor-coordination deficit may account for much of the child's inability to imitate. A child who produces both consonants and vowels generally moves along faster in therapy.

- **Primarily Vowels**

  Vowels are characterized by the placement of the tongue during production. Placement can be **front** to **back** and **high** to **low**. At this level, and for our purposes, we will look at three locations on each placement dimension, front-back vowels and high-low vowels.

high vowels:	/i/ as in *eat*	/u/ as in *who*
front vowels:	/æ/ as in *had*	/o/ as in *over*
low vowels:	/ɑ/ as in *hot*	/ɔ/ as in *fall*

- **Primarily Consonants**

  Consonants can be described in terms of the **place** they are produced, the **manner** in which they are produced, and whether or not the vocal folds are involved to produce **voicing**.

  Place refers to where the tongue is placed in the oral cavity to produce the sound.

front sounds:	/d/ as in *day*	/t/ as in *too*
back sounds:	/g/ as in *gum*	/k/ as in *cat*

Manner refers to whether the sound is produced with a continuous stream of air (a "continuant") or on a short burst of air (a "stop").

continuants:	/s/ as in *see*	/f/ as in *fan*	/ʃ/ as in *shoe*
stops:	/t/ as in *tea*	/d/ as in *dish*	/p/ as in *pop*
	/b/ as in *big*	/tʃ/ as in *chip*	

Voicing refers to whether the sound is voiced or unvoiced (whispered).

unvoiced:	/t/ as in *top*	/k/ as in *kid*	/f/ as in *fill*
	/s/ as in *sit*	/ʃ/ as in *sure*	/p/ as in *pig*
voiced:	/b/ as in *bat*	/d/ as in *dot*	/g/ as in *girl*
	/m/ as in *map*	/l/ as in *log*	/v/ as in *van*

Beyond single speech sounds, children begin producing sounds as single syllables, either as **consonant-vowel (CV) combinations**, such as *ma* or *me*, or as **vowel-consonant (VC) combinations**, such as *eat* or *up*.

What is the prosody of the child's vocalizations?

Prosody of speech refers to the melody of speech, which is determined by pitch, voice quality, and duration of sound. What we perceive is intonation and stress patterns. Indicate the types of pitch and intensity (loudness) the child uses in making any vocalizations or saying any words. Is the pitch monotone, fluctuating, rising, or falling? Is the sound or word produced softly, loudly, or in between?

What is the child's affective state when producing sounds?

Some children produce more sounds when they are angry. Others produce more sounds when they are excited. Still others produce more sounds when they are relaxed.

During what activities does the child produce more sounds?

This is one of the most important questions on the inventory. What is the child doing when he is most vocal or verbal? Is he playing, protesting, teasing, or requesting something? Determine the activities during which the child has a good chance of being vocal. Then incorporate those activities into therapy so that you can start off with a high probability of sounds occurring. When the child vocalizes, reinforce his behavior in order to increase the frequency of the child responding vocally.

Does the child frequently produce any speech sound postures at rest or during play or other activities?

Some children are just not very vocal, but they still have oral postures. If the child has reasonably good muscle tone in his face and does not have chronic nasal congestion, then you have a good chance of eliciting a bilabial (two-lip) sound such as /m/, /p/, or /b/. If, on the other hand, the child has chronic nasal congestion and low muscle tone with an open-mouth posture, you won't want to start with the /m/, /p/, or /b/ sounds since they involve lip muscles. If the child has a hard time breathing and isn't too keen on closing off the airway even for a fraction of a second to produce consonant sounds, then target vowel sounds to start. Here are some postures to look for in your observation:

- lip approximation (ability to bring the lips together)
- lip retraction (corners of mouth retracted as in smiling)
- open mouth (from slightly open to wide open)
- tongue elevation (tongue tip to top teeth or hard palate/gum behind teeth)

What about oral-motor imitation skills?

Oral-motor imitation and exercises are important for acquiring intelligible speech. Oral-motor issues certainly need to be addressed, but oral-motor work often begins with "oral-motor stimulation" to increase the child's awareness of various muscles and how to work them. That's fine, but we need to remember that each child's oral structures come with a child attached.

You want me to talk, but it's hard and I'm not sure I want to do it. Do you really think I will want to talk more if you push, pull, tug, and tap on my face like I am a piece of clay? There is no pleasure in that and I feel powerless.

Children often learn to compensate for many oral-motor challenges if they are given a chance. Try to enable children to use speech to communicate. Initially, make every effort to rely on the child's auditory channel as much as possible. Talk to the child. That is how humans are programmed to learn spoken language, and it's the most efficient learning style for most children.

Jaime's Story

Jaime was referred to me when he was nine years old by a friend of mine who was an occupational therapist. Jaime had sustained a serious head injury at age five. Like many people with a head injury, he often exhibited challenging behavior, and my friend knew I often worked with children with challenging behavior.

I learned from Jaime's mother that his previous speech therapist had introduced signing to him. Apparently Jaime was also being considered for an augmentative device. After spending some time with him, I realized there were some problems with both signing and using an augmentative device. First of all, Jaime's injury left him a triplegic—he only had use of his left arm and hand. Second, Jaime had difficulty with attending and binocular focusing. He could focus one eye or the other, but not both simultaneously. It was hard for him to track objects with his eyes, and I suspected that he had other visual problems. Focusing on any visual display was likely to frustrate him, probably encouraging him to act out with challenging behavior.

Fortunately, Jaime's hearing was reasonably intact. If his hearing was strong, maybe he could learn to use speech, but there would be some problems here, too. Jaime had significant dysarthria (difficulty controlling the muscles needed for speech). He could say approximations of a few words. His speech production was labored, and his intelligibility was poor. Oral-motor work was out of the question at this point. I sensed that if I sat down, pulled on latex gloves, and started giving him "direct stimulation to the oral area," Jaime would communicate to me in no uncertain terms exactly where the door was. Hmm, this would be a real challenge! *(continued on next page)*

I decided to use some sound-stimulation cards with Jaime. These cards showed black-and-white line drawings. I had used the cartoony pictures with a number of children to help them acquire early-developing speech sounds and to increase their phonemic awareness of speech sounds. I said, "Jaime, I want you to look at my silly sound cards. We are going to make these silly sounds." To my delight, he was able to focus visually on the cards and even found them entertaining.

The first time we used the cards, Jaime was able to produce many of the sounds in isolation and had fun doing it. As a former dancer and actress, I decided that if I added a lot of facial expression and some movement, it would take some of the boredom away and make the task of producing speech sounds more appealing.

Jaime produced most of the consonant sounds within a few weeks of introducing the cards. Consonant-vowel combinations and word approximations soon followed. Within twelve months of therapy, Jaime was a full-fledged verbal communicator. His intelligibility continued to improve, as did his mean length of utterance (the number of words he said per vocalization), vocabulary, and conversation skills. At one point, one of Jaime's favorite activities was to take turns with his brothers reciting lines from movies, complete with accents, and seeing who could guess the actor and the movie. From what I understand, Jaime was very good at guessing, and when his turn came to recite a line, he was quite the actor, complete with facial expression, body movement, and accent.

The interesting part is that, in all the time I worked with Jaime, I did almost no direct oral-motor stimulation or exercises. Every now and then I would try "direct stimulation to the oral area," but I decided the risk of anger and frustration wasn't worth it. It is now many years later. Jaime uses spoken language for functional and fun communication. He has a great sense of humor and loves to learn as much as he can about as many things as he can. *Technology* is his newest favorite word.

The Stimulus Inventory: "What He Wants"

Like the sound inventory, the stimulus inventory is extremely important. Children who are non-imitative and nonverbal are usually that way because speech is difficult, not because they are "stubborn." They may have difficulties with either auditory processing and/or motor planning, coordination, and sequencing. Some children may not realize that speech is communication. They may be so distracted by internal or external stimuli that they cannot attend to speech long enough to gain anything from it. Speech may be little more than background noise to these children.

Imitating speech sounds is not an appropriate activity because it is hard for these children to do. If we want them to overcome extremely difficult obstacles, we have to make the payoff worth the effort. The Stimulus Inventory, page 83, should identify those things the child may be interested enough in to overcome difficult obstacles and marshal the attention, motor control and sequencing, and motivation to produce a target sound or syllable upon request.

But there may be a "Catch 22." Some stimuli are so appealing to a child that she cannot organize herself and focus on what it is she is supposed to say. For example, if a child is very hungry, it is difficult for her to focus on a prompt for sound imitation to get the food she wants so much. You may have more success if you make sure the child is interested in the food stimulus, but not so hungry she can't focus and coordinate her movements to produce the desired sound.

Consider the following information as you complete the Stimulus Inventory, page 83, with a child's parent or caregiver:

Preferred Activities

The activities a child likes tell us a lot about his sensorimotor-processing profile. This information may also tell us about the child's attention span and receptive language. If the child loves high action and rough-and-tumble games, then we can generally assume that the child has no gravitational insecurity and can handle his feet being off the ground. If the child likes repetitive or perseverative play, the child may have a limited repertoire of skills to manipulate toys. If a child loves to be held and is clingy, we suspect the child craves deep-pressure input. If the child likes puzzles, we know that some aspects of the child's visual-spatial skills are good.

Certainly there are "preferred" activities that are socially inappropriate and so cannot be allowed, but in 25 years of working with children and adults with severe communication disorders and severely challenging behavior, I have not yet run into a client for whom I could not find some appropriate activity. You just have to be extremely creative and persevere.

Stimulus Inventory

Child _____   Date _____

Information provided by _____

List the child's preferred foods, toys, activities, and places below. Be sure to ask the parent or caregiver to identify the things the child likes currently or has liked in the past.

Preferred Activities

Current _____

_____

Past _____

_____

Preferred Toys

Current _____

_____

Past _____

_____

Preferred Foods (Be sure to ask about food allergies and diet restrictions.)

Current _____

_____

Past _____

_____

Preferred Places

Current _____

_____

Past _____

_____

Preferred Toys

Here are some suggestions for determining and using a child's preferred toys:

- A child who has poor toy manipulation skills may avoid toys that require motor planning, motor coordination, and sequencing. This child probably will avoid assembly toys, such as Legos. The child may have difficulty manipulating toy figures and will probably have difficulty with pretend play.

- A child with sound sensitivity will probably avoid toys that emit sound and prefer toys with no sound output.

- A child with tactile defensiveness may dislike play dough, sand play, and finger painting.

- When we list the toys a child prefers, we may find that there are some features the toys have in common that we didn't realize, thus increasing our stimulus pool.

- It is important to use the toys with features that appeal to children, but you can't use the same toy for too long or the child will become bored with it.

Preferred Foods

For many children, food is the strongest stimulus early on. It is food they are most interested in. Be sure to consider the types of foods the child prefers. Tastes, textures, and colors may all be important. I generally recommend that the parents send in whatever edible items I may use. Document any known food allergies or other diet restrictions.

Preferred Places

Knowing the places the child prefers may give us more information about what activities and toys the child might like. If we know a child loves to go to his grandparents' house, with more questioning, we may find out that there is something the grandparents have that the child absolutely loves that the parents might not even know about.

Pairing Sounds with Stimulus Items: "What He Must Say to Get What He Wants"

The next step is to figure out how to pair specific, high-frequency sounds with foods, objects, or activities the child likes. These sounds will help you develop the child's early core vocabulary. You have to be able to pair sounds with stimulus items that can be shaped into words that can be associated with desired stimulus items: foods, objects, or activities. The goal is for the child to imitate in response to prompts. Remember to select high-frequency sounds that the child produces during pleasurable activities.

An example compilation of the sounds a child produces, the child's preferred stimulus items, target words, and prompts for those words is offered below for your reference.

Sounds the Child Produces	The Child's Preferred Stimulus Items
/i/	Cheetohs
/a/	puzzle
/u/	bubbles
/k/	juice
/d/	See 'n' Say
/m/	music box
/s/	fruit snacks

Here's how to pair these up to prompt the child to say target sounds:

Sound	Item	Word	Prompt
/i/	Cheetohs	"Cheetoh"	"Cheetoh"—"Say 'Eee'."
		"eat"	"Eat"—"Say 'Eee'."
/a/	bubbles	"pop"	"Pop"—"Say 'Ahh'."
	music box	"on"	"On"—"Say 'Ahh'."
/s/	juice	"juice"	"Juice"—"Say 'Sss'."
	See 'n' Say	"See 'n' Say"	"See"—"Say 'Sss'."

Skill: The child imitates one sound consistently.

Description: The child imitates a target sound when given a model and given the prompt "(child's name), say _____."

Materials: Toys, books, games, or foods that the child prefers

Procedure:

1. Position yourself facing the child at eye level.

2. Have the preferred stimulus item within view but out of reach. If possible, position the item near your mouth to increase the likelihood that the child will look at your mouth.

3. Get the child's attention.

4. Prompt the child to say a high-frequency sound from his repertoire: "(child's name), say _____."

5. The child can respond in one of three ways when prompted to "Say _____." The procedures to follow from this point on are determined by the child's response to the prompt for imitation. Example speech-shaping activities are listed after each type of response.

   - The child produces a **correct, imitative response**.

     Prompt: Kevin, here's a ball. Ball. Say "Bah."
     Response: Bah.
     Prompt: Bah. Ball. Here is the ball.

     - Reinforce that production with the object (a ball), lots of social interaction, and praise.

     - Quickly prompt for several more productions of the same sound. Vary stimulus items as necessary, but **not** the target sound. *Bah* can be used to request *baby, book, bubbles, Big Bird,* and many other items. Be creative!

     - Reinforce each correct production in response to a prompt.

     - Target 30 to 50 productions of the first target sound during the first session.

- The child should achieve 80% accuracy in imitation of the first sound before going on to the next sound.

- The child produces an **incorrect response** or an **error sound**.

Prompt:	Kevin, here's a ball. Ball. Say "Bah."
Response:	Eee.
Prompt:	Kevin, here's a ball. Ball. Say "BAAH."
Response:	Eee.
Prompt:	(Imitate the child's error response.) Eee. Kevin, say "Eee."
Response:	Eee.
Prompt:	Kevin. Ball goes up. Whee! Say "Eee."
Response:	Eee.
Prompt:	Great, Kevin! Eee. Here's the ball. Whee!
Response:	(The child reaches for the ball and plays with it briefly.)
Prompt:	Kevin, here's another ball. (Throw the ball up.) Whee! Kevin, say "Eee."
Response:	Eee.
Prompt:	Super, Kevin! Here's the ball. Whee!

- Ignore the error, and prompt for the target sound again with more vocal emphasis.

- If the response after two or three additional prompts is still incorrect, prompt for the incorrect response immediately after the child produces it. Reward correct imitation.

- Reinforce correct responses. You can change the stimulus items, but the prompted sound has to be the same. The target, again, is 80% or higher imitation accuracy.

- The child produces **no sound**, which is considered a **non-response**.

Prompt:	Kevin, here's a ball. Ball. Say "Bah."
Response:	(No sound produced)
Prompt:	Kevin, here's a ball. Ball. Say "Bah."

- Select a food the child likes. Hold it at the child's mouth level, and move it toward the child's mouth. (Be sure to use small bites of food—small enough so that it doesn't take long to consume but large enough so that the child doesn't become angry.)

- As the child opens his mouth to receive the bite, stop just outside his mouth, and say "Ah." Wait with anticipation for his response.

- As the child moves closer to the food, keep it just out of reach, and prompt the child to say "Ah."

- The child will usually vocalize at this point to signal he wants the food. Reinforce any sound with the food and lots of praise.

- Repeat several times, reinforcing vocalizations.

- Prompt again for the sound you have reinforced in steps 4 and 5 (pages 86-87): "Say _____." If the child still doesn't imitate, repeat steps 2 and 3 (page 86).

Tips for Success

- Load the therapy session with as many items as possible so that you can entice the child to produce the target sound. You want the child to produce the sound several times in succession.

- Each production involves innervation of a particular path in the brain. We want that path innervated several times in a row. We are trying to make a path for the child that will be easier to "find" the next time. This strategy decreases the likelihood of the *he said it once and I haven't heard it since* phenomena.

- Remember to use sounds from the child's repertoire. The child may produce them spontaneously during the session. Early in treatment, it is very important to reinforce the child only for prompted responses. Otherwise the child will not successfully learn to listen and produce sounds imitatively.

- Tickle the child briefly to encourage laughing or giggling. Repeat several times. Then move in as though you are going to tickle, and pause just inches away from tickling. In anticipation of the tickling, the child may vocalize laughter or giggling. When he vocalizes, reinforce with tickling and lots of social praise and interaction.

- You could also do some direct stimulation to the lips and prompt for the /m/ target sound.

- You could use sound-activated toys. Connect a toy or a light to a foot switch that you control. If the child vocalizes, reinforce by quickly turning on the light or the toy by using the foot switch. Again, the child sees that sounds have power.

- You could use a microphone. Children often like the sound amplified through a speaker.

Treatment Stage 2 (Type 3 ELD): Activity 2

Skill: The child imitates two sounds consistently.

Description: The child produces a second target sound imitatively without a decrease in proficiency of production of the first target sound.

Materials: Food, toys, activities, or books from the list of the child's preferred stimuli on the Stimulus Inventory, page 83.

Use a different set of stimulus items for the second sound.

Procedure:

1. Select a second target sound that is as different from the first sound in as many features as possible, such as the first sound "mm" and the second sound "ah."

2. Prompt for imitation.

3. If the child imitates the target sound, reinforce with an object and social praise.

4. If the child does not respond, follow the procedure on pages 87-88.

5. If the child produces the first target sound instead of the second one, do not reinforce the child. Prompt and reinforce any sound other than the first target sound.

6. Prompts should be approximately 25% for the "old sound" (the first target sound) and 75% for the "new sound" (the second target sound). If the child decreases his accuracy for imitating the first target sound, then change the prompt ratio to 50% for the first target sound and 50% for the second target sound.

Skill: The child imitates three sounds or syllables consistently.

Description: The child produces one target sound, and then switches to a different target sound when prompted.

Materials: Sets of stimulus items to prompt for up to three different target sounds

Use a different set of stimulus items for each sound.

Procedure:

1. Prompt the child to produce a first target sound in order to get an item she wants. Repeat four more times, using the same or different stimulus items.

2. Prompt the child to produce a second target sound. Repeat four more times.

3. Prompt the child to produce a third target sound. Repeat four more times.

4. Prompt the child to produce the first target sound three times. Repeat for the second and third target sounds, three times each. If the child's accuracy drops and she cannot switch to the new sound, go back to four or five productions of a target sound before switching to the next sound.

5. Prompt for one production of the first target sound, then one production of the second target sound, and then one production of the third target sound, and so forth, until the child can switch to a new sound after only one production. If the child's accuracy decreases, increase to two productions of a sound before changing sounds.

Tip for Success

Structured sound-production sets are extremely important. Often children will produce a sound, a word approximation, or a word, and then not be able to say it again. We want these children to have consistent, high-frequency production so that they don't have difficulty recalling how to produce the sounds.

Treatment Stage 2 (Type 3 ELD): Activity 4

Skill: The child imitates three-to-eight sounds or syllables consistently.

Description: The child produces up to eight different sounds in response to a prompt to get a desired object, activity, or interaction.

Materials: Sets of stimulus items to prompt for up to eight different target sounds

Use a different set of stimulus items for each sound.

Procedure:
1. Prompt for productions of sounds in the child's sound repertoire so the child experiences success.

2. Prompt the child to imitate a new sound from the sound inventory that is different from the sounds in his imitative repertoire. For example, if the first two target sounds or syllables have been consonants or a consonant-vowel combination, you could prompt for a vowel, such as "ah."

3. If the child cannot imitate the new sound after a few prompts, prompt for a different sound.

4. Once the child imitates a new sound, prompt for it four more times in a row:

   Prompt 1: Say "bah" for *ball*. Bah.
   Response: Bah.
   Prompt 2: That's right! Ball. Say "bah" for *ball*. Bah.
   Response: Bah.
   Prompt 3: Yes, you said "Bah." Ball. Here's the ball. Here is another ball. Say "Bah."
   Response: Bah.
   Prompt 4: Bah. Yes, ball. Here it is. Oh, look, another ball for you! Say "Bah."
   Response: Bah.
   Prompt 5: Wow, here it is! Look! Here are some bubbles. Say "Bah."
   Response: Bah.

5. Continue to prompt for the "old" sounds or syllables while working on each new one. Fifty percent of the prompts should be for the "new" sound, and 50% should be for the old sounds.

Skill: The child produces single-syllable word approximations and words.

Description: The child expands her repertoire of sounds and syllables to word approximations and single-syllable words.

Materials: Sets of stimulus items to prompt for 10-15 syllables or word approximations

Procedure:
1. Prompt for production of sounds and syllables in the child's repertoire, using preferred stimulus items from the Stimulus Inventory, page 83.

2. Probe for expansion of existing sound and syllables by presenting each sound and syllable with an additional phoneme or syllable, placing emphasis on the additional phonemes or syllable. Try using tactile and visual cues to cue production. For example, I often cue /t/ or /d/ by pairing the sound with a tap to the forearm with an index finger. I cue production of /s/ with running my index finger down my arm as I produce the sound. I hold my index finger to my lips to cue the production of /ʃ/, the "quiet sound."

Target Word	Child's Approximation	Expanded Target
eat	ee	eeT
pop	pa	poP
chip	ip	CHip
candy	dee	can-DY
open	o	o-PEN
book	bah	boo-K
tickle	k-k-k	Tika-Tika
boom	boo	booM

Tip for Success

Children who do not have significant verbal apraxia will generally move quickly through this treatment phase. By this point, many children have learned how to learn language and are producing words they have not been taught. If children have difficulty synthesizing sounds and are not acquiring words rapidly on their own, then more direct oral-motor treatment and/or apraxia treatment may be necessary.

Treatment Stage 2 (Type 3 ELD): Activity 6

Skill: The child produces words spontaneously.

Description: The child learns to produce words without a verbal model or visual or gestural cues.

Materials: Sets of stimulus items to prompt for up to ten different words

Procedure:
1. Select stimulus items that the child enjoys and that have the highest rate of correct word imitations.

2. Prompt by asking "What do you want?" or "What is this?" with the stimulus in the child's field of vision but out of reach.

3. Give only as much cueing as necessary for the child to give the correct production.

Cueing Hierarchy

Most Prompt (word) + model + tactile and/or gesture or visual cue

Prompt (initial sound cue) + tactile and/or gesture or visual cue

Prompt + tactile and/or gesture or visual cue

Prompt

Least No cues, labels, or requests without prompt

---

4. Reinforce the child's spontaneous word productions.

Tip for Success

It is very important to fade cues and models as soon as possible so that the child does not become dependent upon them.

Chapter 6

Treatment Stage 3: Then Sentences

After children acquire a core vocabulary, the next treatment stage involves learning to sequence words into phrases and sentences. During this treatment stage, the principles of *pleasure, power, play,* and *practice* (see pages 57-60), still hold true. Children will be most motivated to learn language that has a strong sensorimotor component and/or a strong emotional component. By the time children reach this stage, they are usually well aware of (or soon will be aware of) the power of words.

During the early phase of Treatment Stage 3, we begin to see the child with expressive language disorder (ELD), regardless of the type, demonstrating that he has learned how to "learn language." He begins to use words that have not been targeted in therapy and acquires words rapidly. Some parents have commented that it's almost as though we have tapped into the child's natural ability to learn language.

Early word combinations represent a variety of semantic-grammatic relations. We want to make sure that we focus on as many of these as possible in therapy. Here are some early word combinations that occur the most frequently:

Grammar/Semantic Functions	Two-word Combinations
Agent + action	Baby eat.
Action + object	Eat cookie.
Agent + object	Mommy shoe.
Entity + attribute	Shoe wet.
Demonstrative + entity	There doggie.
Noun + locative	Mommy car.
Verb + locative	Go outside.
Recurrence	More juice.
Possessor + possession	Daddy hat.
Nonexistence	Cookie all gone. (*all gone* = one word)
Disappearance	Bye-bye, Daddy.
Rejection	No nite-nite.
Denial	No tired.

Grammar/Semantic Functions	**Three-word Combinations**
Agent + action + object	Baby eat cookie.

Next, children begin to produce some early sentences with carrier phrases. These carrier phrases typically include *I want, I see, I have,* and *I like*. Children use these phrases to produce sentences such as *I want juice* or *I see Daddy*.

Another early sentence structure includes *-ing* verb forms, such as *Daddy is eating fries*. At first, children may omit the word *is* from these sentences: *Daddy eating fries*.

Treatment Stage 3 is a very exciting phase for the child. During this phase, the child begins to use words in combinations to describe what he sees and feels in his world. People and things occupy places in his life: people (agents) doing things (actions). Sometimes *Baby is here*. Sometimes *Barney is there*. Sometimes people and things are *on*; then they fall *off*. They are *in, under,* or *behind*. People can be *happy, sad,* and *mad*. The child has begun to learn with language, and he can begin to exercise more control over the people and events in his life: *No nite-nite* and *More cookie*. Treatment Stage 3 lays the foundation for the growth of language from simple to sophisticated.

Treatment Stage 3: Activity 1

Skill: The child produces multi-word utterances during play with objects.

Description: The child produces phrases and sentences during familiar routines involving toys.

Materials: Favorite, familiar toys, such as balls, bubbles, shape sorters, or puzzles

Procedure:

1. Engage the child in a familiar play routine with a toy.

2. Model expanded utterances as you and the child play, using words from the child's repertoire and placing special vocal emphasis on the added words. For instance, if the child says "Car," you could model "Car GO" as you push the car away. Here are some example phrases and sentences to model for this activity:

Two-word Combinations

Car vroom!	No all done. (*All done* functions as one word.)
Ball in.	More ball.
Bye-bye, Barney.	My bubbles.

Three-word Combinations

Mommy pop bubble.

Early Sentences

I want puzzle.
I see circle.
I have bubbles.
Mickey (is) popping bubbles.

You could also add a gesture or a special movement to emphasize the added word. Make it fun and interesting!

3. Pause and wait with anticipation for the child to produce the modeled utterance.

4. If the child does not respond or still produces a single-word response, you may have to prompt for the child to imitate your production. See the example on the following page:

Prompt: Car GO!
Response: Car
Prompt: Danny say, "Car GO!"
Response: Car GO!

Tips for Children with Type 2 or Type 3 ELD

• Some children with Type 2 ELD and most with Type 3 ELD require extensive use of prompted imitation and visual or gestural cues to produce multi-word utterances.

• Sometimes making the activity a little more structured and having the child produce phrases with only one word changing is helpful. For example, during a shape-sorting activity, the child could say "Bye-bye" to each shape as it disappears into the shape sorter. (*Bye-bye, circle; Bye-bye, triangle;* etc.)

Treatment Stage 3: Activity 2

Skill: The child produces multi-word utterances during pretend play.

Description: The child produces phrases and sentences during familiar, symbolic-play activities.

Materials:

toy figures	clothing
toy furniture	toy vehicles
toy house	food

Procedure:

1. Engage the child in familiar, symbolic-play schemas, such as a birthday party or putting a baby to bed.

2. Model expanded utterances during play, using words from the child's repertoire and placing special vocal emphasis on the added words. For example, if the child says "Baby" while putting a baby to bed, you could model "Baby SLEEP." If the child says "Sleep" while putting the baby to bed, you can add "Baby, BABY sleep."

   You could also add a gesture or a special movement to emphasize the added word, such as resting your head on your hands as if you're laying your head on a pillow as you emphasize the word *sleep*. Make it fun and interesting!

   Here are some example phrases and sentences to model for this activity:

   ### Two-word Combinations

Barney eat.	Pooh there.
Silly Barney.	Uh-oh, Pooh.
No Baby Bop.	Nite-nite, baby.

   ### Three-word Combinations

   Barney eat apple.

   ### Early Sentences

   I want (the) car.
   I see (a) baby.
   I like Barney.
   Barney (is) climbing up.

3. Pause and wait with anticipation for the child to produce the modeled utterance.

4. If the child does not respond or still produces a single-word response, you may have to prompt for the child to imitate your production:

Prompt:	Baby SLEEP.
Response:	Sleep.
Prompt:	Kevin, say "Baby SLEEP."
Response:	Baby SLEEP.

Tips for Children with Type 2 or Type 3 ELD

- Children with Type 2 or Type 3 ELD may have difficulty with motor coordination and sequencing and, therefore, find symbolic play with toy figures difficult. Make sure the doors of toy buildings, etc., are open enough for children to move figures in and out easily.

- If you are using a toy house, try to use one with the furniture "attached" or molded into the design of the house so the children do not have to hold the figure and the furniture at the same time.

- Dressing dolls is difficult for some children with motor-planning, coordination, and sequencing problems. Usually pretending to feed a baby with a bottle is easier than using eating utensils. Make sure the bottle is easy to hold and the bottle's destination, the baby's mouth, is easy to see.

- Use favorite commercial characters or stuffed animals if the child is not interested in mommy, daddy, or baby figures.

Treatment Stage 3: Activity 3

Skill: The child produces multi-word utterances during outside play.

Description: The child produces phrases and sentences during active play outside on a playground or in a play area.

Materials: Toys and equipment appropriate for outside play, such as the following:

tricycles	balls
sand toys	jungle gym
slide	swing
seesaw	playhouse

Procedure:
1. Involve the child in play on outdoor equipment or with outdoor toys.

2. Model expanded utterances during familiar, easy play. Do not model or prompt for expanded language if the child is engaged in play with equipment or toys that are new or difficult for the child to manage. Make sure the language matches the action of the play in content and, if possible, tempo, such as *Up, up, up,* (pause) *slide down.*

   Here are some example phrases and sentences to model for this activity:

   Two-word Combinations

Go up	More swing
My ball	Play ball
No slide	Here ball

   Three-word Combinations

   Ball go up.

   Early Sentences

   I want ball.
   I have (the) bubbles.
   I like outside.
   Mommy (is) swinging high.

3. Pause and wait with anticipation for the child to produce the modeled utterance.

4. If the child does not respond or still produces a single-word response, you may have to prompt for imitation:

Prompt: Go UP.
Response: Go.
Prompt: Amy, say "Go UP."
Response: Go UP.

Tips for Children with Type 2 or Type 3 ELD

- Remember that some children with Type 2 or Type 3 ELD have gravitational insecurity and don't like having their feet off the ground. Use a slide or a jungle gym with caution with these children.

- "Chase" is an easy, fun game for most children with Type 2 or Type 3 ELD. Make sure that sometimes they are the "chasers," and sometimes they are the "chasees."

- Blowing bubbles is also a fun, easy game for children with Type 2 or Type 3 ELD.

Treatment Stage 3: Activity 4

Skill: The child produces multi-word utterances during snacks and meals.

Description: The child uses early-developing phrases and sentences to request, comment, refuse, and label during snack preparation, distribution, consumption, and cleanup.

Materials: Snack time items that may include the following:

snack foods	regular mealtime foods
beverages	napkins
cups	place mats
name cards	

Procedure: 1. During routine snack or mealtimes, model expanded language for the child. Here are some example phrases and sentences to model for this activity:

Two-word Combinations

Milk cold.	There juice.
Uh-oh, milk.	Cookie (on) table.
More juice.	All done juice.

Three-word Combinations

I eat cookie.

Early Sentences

I like juice.
I see (an) apple.
I have milk.
I want more.
Baby (is) eating cracker.

Among the foods you offer, include some that the child does not like to give him opportunities to refuse. You could also have foods with interesting textures or shapes that will encourage the child to comment. Arrange the foods in an interesting display to entice the child to make comments.

2. Model expanded utterances during preparation, consumption, and cleanup. Use vocal emphasis and/or gestures as you say the added words. For example, roll and pat play dough as you say "Roll and pat." Touch a pretend cookie and say "Cookie hot!" with

appropriate facial expression. Pretend to eat a cookie, saying "Cookie yummy." Say "Napkin away" as you throw a napkin into a wastebasket.

3. Pause and wait with anticipation for the child to say something.

4. If the child does not respond or still produces a single-word response, you may have to prompt the child to imitate your comment:

Prompt:	Cookie yummy.
Response:	Yummy.
Prompt:	Carrie, say "COOKIE yummy!"
Response:	Cookie yummy!

Tips for Children with Type 2 or Type 3 ELD

• Often fun, descriptive words, such as *sticky, wet, cold, gooey, crunchy,* and *yummy,* are appealing and more likely to be produced by children with Type 2 or Type 3 ELD.

• Some children with Type 2 or Type 3 ELD are more motivated to produce speech to request foods they prefer. Be sure to have several food and beverage choices so that the child has opportunities to label and make requests.

• Serve small portions of food so that the child has to make requests more often.

• Food preparations that involve "hands on" activity, such as rolling, patting, pouring, cutting, squeezing, pulling, and dropping, are great for children with Type 2 or Type 3 ELD if these children are not tactilely defensive. The sounds of the words and the accompanying rhythm and movement gets and keeps their attention and increases the likelihood that they will recall and produce the expanded utterances.

Skill: The child produces multi-word utterances during movement and music activities.

Description: During music and movement activities, the child produces early phrase and sentence forms to request, comment, refuse, and/or greet.

Materials: Tape-recorded music
Musical instruments

Procedure: 1. During activities with familiar songs and music, model expanded utterances. Here are some example phrases and sentences to model for this activity:

Two-word Combinations

Go march.	No drum.
Music on.	My music.
Music loud.	Music there.

Three-word Combinations

My turn drum.

Early Sentences

I like music.
I have (a) drum.
I want (the) piano.
Daddy (is) playing music.

During games such as "Simon Says," the child can be Simon and give commands. The child can also make verbal choices of games, instruments, finger plays, songs, and music.

2. Model expanded utterances with vocal and/or gestural emphasis on the added word. For example, say "Go march!" as you demonstrate marching around the room. If the music is loud, point to the music source, then cover your ears; smile and keep your facial expression positive so the child doesn't fear the music is loud enough to hurt your ears.

3. Pause and wait with anticipation for the child's production.

4. If the child does not respond or produces only a single-word response, you may have to provide a model and prompt for imitation:

Prompt: Music off.
Response: Off.
Prompt: Jason, say "MUSIC off."
Response: Music off.

Tips for Children with Type 2 or Type 3 ELD

- Make sure the child has no auditory hypersensitivity to the level of loudness and/or the type of music. Some children are bothered more by the type of music than the loudness of the music.

- Children with motor-planning and coordination problems may need extra assistance in order to play musical instruments. They may need physical assistance or more time to process before they produce specific movements or movement patterns.

- Some children with Type 2 or Type 3 ELD may find it difficult to participate in an activity and produce language at the same time. These children may require contingent reinforcement using primary reinforcers, such as food. Most children learn to enjoy the activities themselves enough to fade any primary reinforcers that have been used initially. Fade these reinforcers as soon as participating in music and movement activities alone is reinforcing enough to retain the child's interest.

Skill: The child produces multi-word utterances during art time.

Description: During art activities, the child uses early-developing phrases and sentences for a variety of communicative intentions, such as commenting, requesting, labeling, refusing, denying, and calling for attention.

Materials: Age-appropriate art materials, such as the following:

paint	paper
sponge shapes	brushes
crayons	clay
craft dough	glue
scissors	

Procedure: 1. Engage the child in a familiar, favorite art activity.

2. Model expanded utterances, using vocabulary familiar to the child. Use as many fun words as possible. Add movement, gesture, and vocal emphasis to the added words. Here are some example phrases and sentences to model for this activity:

Two-word Combinations

Paint wet.	No color.
My paint.	I cut.
Paper there.	Look, (it's) pretty!

Three-word Combinations

Mommy paint picture.

Early Sentences

I see (the) picture.
I have paint.
I like paint.
I want paper.
Mommy (is) painting (a) picture.

3. Pause and wait with anticipation for the child to produce the targeted phrase or sentence.

4. If the child does not respond or produces a single-word utterance, model the longer utterance and prompt the child to imitate:

Prompt: Paint wet.
Response: Paint.
Prompt: Michael, say "PAINT wet."
Response: Paint wet.

Tips for Children with Type 2 or Type 3 ELD

- Remember, many children with Type 2 ELD and most with Type 3 ELD have some tactile defensiveness. For language production purposes, with the exception of refusal, our goal is not to make the child less tactilely defensive. It is to have him produce longer utterances during an enjoyable art activity.

- Many children with Type 2 or Type 3 ELD really enjoy sensory-loaded words, such as *sticky* and *squishy*.

- Remember, children with Type 2 or Type 3 ELD may have motor-planning, coordination, and sequencing problems. Make sure the activity you choose is not too challenging motorically, or you'll get a lot of focus on the motor aspects of the activity and very little on the language and communication aspects.

Treatment Stage 3: Activity 7

Skill:　　　　　The child produces multi-word utterances during story time.

Description:　　During story-reading or story-telling time, the child produces early phrase and sentence forms to request, comment, refuse, deny, and label.

Materials:　　　Select books with vocabulary familiar to the child. They should have simple text with rhyming words and the same number of syllables per line. The books should have as many "fun words" as possible. You can also use props to add interest to the story. Here is a list of stories that work well for this activity:

Golden Books, Inc.: Road to Reading, Mile 1
Dancing Dinos by Sally Lucas
Hiccup by Taylor Jordan
Hot Dog by Molly Coxe
I Like Stars by Margaret Wise Brown

DK Family Learning: First Steps to Reading
Be Quiet! by Elspeth Graham
Hold On! by Elspeth Graham

Scholastic, Inc.: Read With Me Cartwheel Books
Here Comes the Snow by Angela Shelf Medearis

Procedure:　　1. Read or tell a story to the child. Use enthusiastic animation and vocal emphasis to make the story interesting. If necessary, do not read the text as printed. Instead, adapt the story to the child's vocabulary and interests.

2. Prompt the child for multi-word utterances. Here are some example phrases and sentences to model for this activity:

Two-word Combinations

Open book.	More book.
Book chair.	No read.
My book?	Sad story.

Three-word Combinations

Barney read book.

Early Sentences

> I want (that) book.
> I like (the) story.
> I see Barney.
> Mommy (is) reading (the) book.

3. If the child does not respond or gives a single-word response, provide a model and prompt the child for imitation:

Prompt: Open book.
Response: Open.
Prompt: Mory, say "Open BOOK."
Response: Open book.

Tips for Children with Type 2 or Type 3 ELD

- Some children with Type 2 ELD and many with Type 3 ELD only like story time when they can hold and "read" the book themselves. If that happens, you can try to shape the child's behavior to allowing the adult to read books. Sometimes it helps to designate books as an "I read" book or a "you read" book. Another option is for the adult to read the first page, and then give the book to the child. The next time, the adult reads the first two pages, and then gives the book to the child. Each time, the adult reads an additional page before handing the book over to the child.

- Books with texture and "flaps" sometimes appeal to children with Type 2 or Type 3 ELD.

- Many children with Type 2 or Type 3 ELD like stories about puppies and babies.

- Many children with Type 2 or Type 3 ELD prefer storybooks with photos rather than illustrations.

- Sometimes children with Type 2 or Type 3 ELD also prefer stories that show a variety of emotions, including sad, mad, and happy. They also like "uh-oh" photos where someone has made a mess or a mistake.

- Be especially careful with the level of animation you add to a story in terms of your movement, facial expression, and voice quality and intensity. Some children with Type 2 or Type 3 ELD appear to have difficulty processing auditory and visual stimuli simultaneously, particularly if there is a high level of animation.

Treatment Stage 3: Activity 8

Skill:	The child produces multi-word utterances during cleanup and transitions to other activities.
Description:	The child produces early phrase and sentence forms to label, comment, request, respond, and seek attention during pick-up and put-away activities.
Materials:	books toys art materials musical instruments other items that must be put away upon completing an activity

Procedure:

1. At the close of an activity, give the child choices of items to put away. Ask the child where things go.

2. Model correct, expanded utterances if the child uses single-word responses. Here are some example phrases and sentences to model for this activity:

Two-word Combinations

Baby away.	All done puzzle.
No away.	In box.
My car.	Clean table.

Three-word Combinations

Baby hold toy.
Put in box.

Early Sentences

I see puzzle.
I want (the) book.
I like (the) baby.
Daddy (is) cleaning (the) table.

3. Pause and wait with anticipation for the child to produce target utterances.

4. Prompt for imitation if the child does not respond or continues to produce single-word responses:

Prompt:	Book away.
Response:	Away.
Prompt:	Katie, say "BOOK away."
Response:	Book away.

The Source for Expressive Language Delay
Chapter 6—Treatment Stage 3: Then Sentences   110   Copyright © 2003 LinguiSystems, Inc.

Tips for Children with Type 2 or Type 3 ELD

- Sometimes children with Type 2 or Type 3 ELD resist changing from one activity to another. Give the children warnings that cleanup is in _____ minutes. A picture schedule that includes "cleanup" is sometimes helpful. You can also set a timer as a signal to clean up.

- Make cleanup as fun and interesting as possible.

- Remember that children with motor-planning, coordination, or sequencing difficulties may have difficulty with cleanup tasks such as holding a container in one hand and sliding a toy into it with the other. Baskets and bins are sometimes better for storing toys for these children.

- Children with Type 2 or Type 3 ELD are often good at labeling or naming items but not at naming actions (verbs) or descriptive terms (adjectives and adverbs). Make sure to target a variety of communicative intentions as you model expanded utterances.

Treatment Stage 3: Activity 9

Skill: The child produces multi-word utterances during self-care activities.

Description: The child produces early phrases and sentences to communicate a variety of intentions, such as labeling, commenting, requesting, responding, protesting, and gaining attention during self-care activities, such as dressing, toileting, teeth brushing, hand washing, and bathing.

Materials: No specific materials

Procedure:
1. During routine, familiar, and preferred self-care activities, model expanded utterances. Here are some example phrases and sentences to model for this activity:

Two-word Combinations

Brush teeth.	My soap.
Hands wet.	Cup there.
No potty.	All done potty.

Three-word Combinations

Barney want soap.

Early Sentences

I see cup.
I have soap.
I like bubbles.
Baby (is) taking (a) bath.

2. Pause and wait with anticipation for the child to produce the modeled utterance. Cue the production with a gesture or movement.

3. If the child does not respond or responds in single-word utterances, provide a model, and prompt the child to imitate longer utterances:

Prompt:	Cup there.
Response:	Cup.
Prompt:	Brendan, say "Cup THERE."
Response:	Cup there.

Tips for Children with Type 2 or Type 3 ELD

- Some children with Type 2 ELD and many with Type 3 ELD have difficulty with the motor-planning, coordination, and sequencing demands of many self-care skills.

- Sometimes sequence pictures depicting the appropriate sequence for a self-care task are beneficial. These picture sequences can be stimuli for language production as well. For example, hand washing could have photos or illustrations showing the steps in the sequence with captions that the child could say, such as those on the following two pages.

Sequence Pictures

Use these pictures to prompt for simple phrases and sentences during hand washing.

Water on.

Hands wet.

Soap on.

Rub and scrub.

Sequence Pictures, *continued*

Use these pictures to prompt for simple phrases and sentences during hand washing.

Rinse and shake.

Paper pull.

Pat and dry.

All done!

Treatment Stage 3: Activity 10

Skill: The child produces multi-word utterances during social play.

Description: The child produces early phrase and sentence forms during social games and routines with adults and children to communicate a variety of intentions, such as labeling, commenting, requesting, responding, and seeking attention.

Materials: No specific materials; scarves and blankets are fun for playing variations of "Peekaboo."

Procedure:

1. Engage the child in favorite, familiar social games and routines.

2. Model correct, expanded utterances. Here are some example phrases and sentences to model for this activity:

   Two-word Combinations

   Silly Daddy.   Tickle tummy!
   Mommy pillow.   Look, Mommy!
   No tickle.   My tummy.

   Three-word Combinations

   Daddy tickle tummy.

   Early Sentences

   I see you.
   I want (to) play.
   I love you.
   Mommy (is) hugging Daddy.

3. Pause and wait with anticipation for the child to produce the modeled utterances.

4. Prompt for imitation if the child does not respond or continues to produce single-word responses:

   Prompt: Tickle tummy.
   Response: Tummy.
   Prompt: Sandy, say "TICKLE tummy."
   Response: Tickle tummy.

Tips for Children with Type 2 or Type 3 ELD

- Be persistent, even if children with Type 2 or Type 3 ELD resist interacting.

- Many children with Type 2 or Type 3 ELD really enjoy tickling if they can see it coming and if you cue it with a sound.

- Try to avoid using food as reinforcers. The purpose of this activity is to connect with the child emotionally. Play and engagement stimulate language.

Chapter 7

Treatment Stage 4: Language Grows Up

During this stage, children with expressive language delay (ELD) move beyond early fun, functional communication to develop elaborated, sophisticated language. They begin to use grammatical sentences and to participate in meaningful conversations. They learn to formulate logical narratives to explain how to do something or to tell what happened. Children learn to retell stories they have heard. They begin to relate their experiences to others. They learn to verbally problem-solve. They begin to discuss their feelings and emotions. During Treatment Stage 4, children acquire the repertoire of sophisticated language that will, hopefully, fully support the breadth and depth of their social-emotional and cognitive development.

The activities in this chapter are divided into three sections: Grammar (pages 125-135), Pre-Discourse (pages 136-144), and Discourse (pages 145-157). The activities within each section are arranged developmentally within each section, but you may address more than one section simultaneously. A discussion of each section follows.

Grammar

Mastering **grammar**, the system that governs word order and relationships in sentences, allows children to understand and convey information accurately and efficiently. In order to develop appropriate grammar to discuss time relationships, children need to understand and use verb tenses correctly. They need to use the past tense to talk about things that have happened. They need to use the future tense to predict outcomes. They need to produce questions to get information and to clarify information. They need to have noun-verb agreement and correct pronoun comprehension and usage in order to understand and convey information clearly and accurately.

Pre-Discourse

Pre-discourse activities focus on the language skills that foster learning and problem-solving. Children need to look at something in their world and be able to understand and verbalize what they see. What does it look like? What does it sound like, feel like, taste like? How is it alike or different from other things? What are its features or attributes? What does it do? How do we use it? What are its parts? What is it made of? Pre-discourse language skills help children to organize, understand, and describe their world.

Discourse

When we begin our treatment journey with a child with ELD, **discourse**, the orderly exchange of ideas, is the destination we hope the child will reach. With adequate grammar and language skills to describe their world and how things are used and are related, children can begin to use language to share their own experiences. They can use language to retell stories or generate stories of their own. They can express their feeling and emotions. They can use language to solve problems and to make decisions about what is right or wrong.

Vertical Language Learning

Learning language is very hard for children with ELD, particularly Types 2 and 3 ELD. We must make sure that what we teach each child is highly relevant, meaningful, and memorable or fun for that child. We must give her as much language as possible to do as many things as possible to communicate with others about the people, places, events, and emotions in her life. How do we give a child so much when language is so hard to learn?

One way to do this is called *vertical language learning.* We establish a base of core, critical communication first, based on what's most relevant, meaningful, and engaging to each particular child. As treatment progresses over time, we expand this core of language. The closer or more "vertically" we adhere to this core language, the higher the payoff for the child in understanding others and expressing herself. The diagram on page 120 illustrates this principle.

Vertical language learning recognizes that X amount of effort goes into learning a new word, concept, or element of language. We want to make sure that after a child puts forth 100X, she can do lots of things with that language. How we can distribute the 100X of effort? Suppose the child spends 40X of effort learning different zoo animals, farm animals, fruits, vegetables, and foods. Then the child spends another 40X of language-learning effort learning 35 different verbs and five different position concepts and 20X learning ten colors, six different shapes, and four descriptors (*rough, smooth, big,* and *little*). For 100X of effort, does the child have broader, more powerful language skills than a child who expended 40X to learn eight favorite and familiar animals, ten favorite foods, eight familiar actions, eight colors, four shapes, and *big* and *little*? Not really. How could that effort be better spent for the child?

Suppose after the initial 40X of effort, the next 60X was spent on learning some early past-tense verbs, more-meaningful descriptors (*wet, sticky, heavy*), emotions (*happy, sad, mad*), and early question words, including *where, who,* and *what.* Maybe the child could learn some future tense. Maybe she could learn comparison language and negation. In other words, instead of learning a lot of somewhat-meaningful language, she would learn a few highly-meaningful elements of many more areas of language. Furthermore, because what we would teach would be highly meaningful to the child, she would learn faster and more easily.

Vertical Language Learning

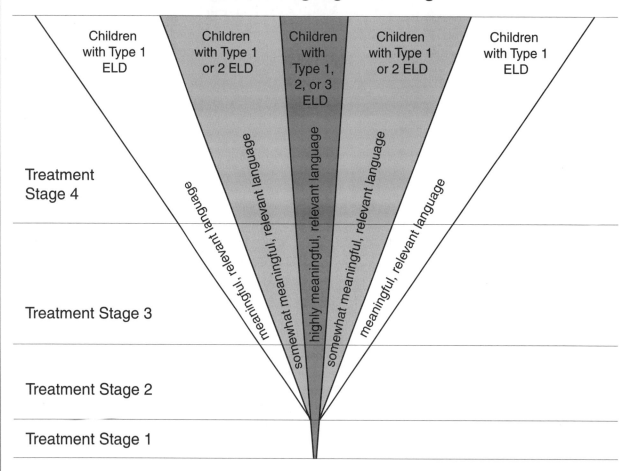

I currently work with children in Trainable Mentally Handicapped classrooms, using past and future tense, recognizing absurdities, using deductive and inductive reasoning, comparing and contrasting, verbally problem-solving, demonstrating sequential thinking, retelling stories, predicting outcomes, etc. They don't necessarily have extensive vocabularies, but what they learn, they use a lot, and it provides them personal power and pleasure. The language they have learned serves as the basis for higher-level learning. With just 50 nouns, ten actions words, a few meaningful descriptors, and a few position concepts, these children have enough language sophistication to facilitate a wide range of higher-level cognitive skills. Moreover, they have mastered the tools that enable them to continue to expand their language learning.

We need to select what we teach children carefully to give them the best possible language "bang" for the effort they put forth. Children will achieve higher language learning if the treatment content and vocabulary are highly relevant and meaningful; they must evoke both pleasure and power for the child. Neutral or irrelevant training doesn't motivate children with ELD to learn, use, or remember language.

When children are encouraged to use language to express meaningful ideas about meaningful people and characters, they can demonstrate some surprising language capabilities. During a one-month period, for example, Michael, a six-year-old child with Type 3 ELD, began the part of his language-learning journey that leads from simple to sophisticated language. Using a jigglypuff Pokeman character as the subject, Michael moved from generating simple sentences describing action to producing simple stories that included early logical and analytical thinking.

Samples of Michael's work during each step in the process are reproduced below. Lori, a graduate student in speech pathology, worked with Michael during these activities. Her description of what occurred during each step is provided for clarification.

Step 1
Jan. 27-28

Michael repeatedly drew a jigglypuff character from Pokemon. To make this a functional activity and increase language usage, I drew pictures of jigglypuffs along with things Michael enjoys and is familiar with, such as a pizza, a Coke, a trampoline, and a swimming pool. After I drew the picture, I prompted Michael to tell me a story based on the picture.

Before beginning this writing process, Michael only labeled nouns and actions in pictures. He didn't connect them to form complete sentences or thoughts. Also, he didn't talk about abstract concepts, such as feelings.

Through scaffolding and expansion, Michael and I wrote a "story" using nouns, adjectives, functor words (*the, is,* and *a*), and verbs of various tenses (present progressive, present, and past) connected in a complete sentence. I modeled the writing process while Michael told me what to write. For example, if Michael said "Jigglypuff eat pizza," I probed with "What is the jigglypuff doing? The jigglypuff is _____" or "What did the jigglypuff do? The jigglypuff _____." Then I expanded and asked "How did it taste?" or "How does he feel when he eats pizza?" to get a response that included emotion. Our story follows:

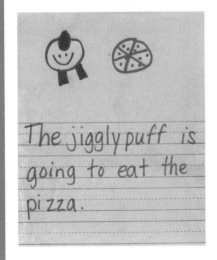

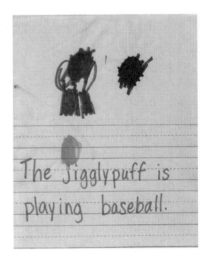

Step 2
Feb. 3-4

I prompted Michael to draw characters doing familiar actions and involved in familiar situations. Then I prompted him to tell me the story. I modeled writing, including sounding out words phonetically as I wrote the letters of the words. Two pages from the story are reproduced below:

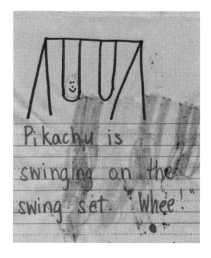

Step 3
Feb. 8-11

Two weeks later, Michael independently drew a picture of a jigglypuff and a pizza, then wrote a letter string describing the pictures. Next, Michael and I began drawing pictures together. He began to write stories based on the pictures. He also began to sound out words as he wrote the letters. He included some pictures within his letter strings, producing draw-write combinations. At this point, he represented most words with one or two letters. The story is pictured on the next page:

The jigglypuff eat.
Taste good.

Michael independently wrote:
    JP = jigglypuff
    The = The
    a = eat
    t = taste
    gb = good

The jigglypuff eat cake
and drink Coke.

Michael independently wrote:
    jgp = jigglypuff
    a = eat
    cc = cake
    g = drink
    picture of Coke = Coke

Pikachu is swimming. It
is fun.

Michael independently wrote:
    Pg = Picachu
    is = is
    swm = swimming
    ti = it
    is = is
    fn = fun

Step 4
Feb. 17-18

I transitioned Michael to more realistic drawings, such as boys and
dinosaurs. I asked him to name the boys and dinosaurs. He named a
boy *George,* who is his favorite friend in school. He named dinosaurs
Johnosauraus and *Batosauraus*. He was learning about dinosaurs in
school that week and made the logical inference that dinosaurs have
names that end in -*sauraus*. This connection represents abstract, analytical
thinking. In this stage, Michael also drew and wrote a story involving a
compound subject and a compound predicate. Here is his story:

Ashe and jigglypuff drink Coke and
eat pizza. It tastes good. Yummy.

Michael independently wrote:
    The = The
    a = Ashee
    jpf = jigglypuff
    gg = drink
    coc = Coke
    pc = pizza
    t = taste
    g = good
    M = yummy

George plays skateboard.

Michael independently wrote:
  girg = George
  plae = play
  sb = skateboard

Step 5
Feb. 25

I began to use the drawings and stories to talk about emotions and inferencing with Michael. I drew pictures in which there were two characters with different emotions, *happy* and *sad*. I then asked, "Michael, why is one happy and one sad?" Through scaffolding, we came up with an idea about why one is happy and one is sad.

Ashe is happy because he is eating pizza. Jigglypuff is sad because his fell on the floor.

Ashe is sad because he spilled his coke. Jigglypuff is happy because he has a coke.

To extend this idea, I drew a picture of a jigglypuff with a bloody knee, standing next to a bicycle. I asked Michael to tell me a story. He expressed the ideas of *jigglypuff, boo-boo on knee,* and *ouch.* He didn't, however, make the inference that the jigglypuff fell off the bike, and that's why he has a hurt knee. I am now trying to teach Michael to draw inferences from pictures and situations by looking at all components of a scene and then forming logical conclusions.

Ashe is crying because he has a boo-boo on his knee. He fell off his bicycle.

Treatment Stage 4: Activity 1

Skill: The child produces past-tense verb forms.

Description: The child produces early-developing regular and irregular past-tense verb forms in sentences.

Materials: Props for pretend play
                   Action photos depicting past-tense verbs
                   Books depicting past-tense activities

Procedure: 1. Model target past-tense verb forms while engaging in play. The play activity can involve gross-motor movements or pretend play with toy characters. Be sure to select verb forms that are very familiar to the child and have high use in daily life.

                   2. Give special vocal emphasis to the past-tense verb as you say it.

                   3. Perform the action yourself or with a toy character, and prompt the child by saying "What **did** I **do**?" or "What **happened**?"

                   4. If the child does not respond or seems confused, model the correct response.

Tips for Children with Type 2 or Type 3 ELD

- The concept of past tense is very difficult for many children with Type 2 or Type 3 ELD. These children are okay with the "here and now," but have great difficulty with the "then and there." For many of these children, "out of sight" is literally "out of mind." Provide as many visual cues as possible. One easy way to teach the concept of past tense is to place an object on the table, have the child close his eyes, take it away, and ask, "What was there?" or "What's gone?"

- Certain past-tense action verbs, such as *ate, broke, fell,* and *drew,* appear to be easier to learn than others. Using action words that have a strong visual contrast between the present tense and past tense and a strong emotional component may make learning easier. For example, the difference between eating popcorn and an empty bowl and a sad face because someone **ate** it all is easier for children to remember.

Treatment Stage 4: Activity 2

Skill: The child states what will happen in the future.

Description: The child produces verb forms that indicate future occurrences, including *going to* and *will*, in sentences.

Materials: Props and action figures
Photos depicting something that will happen
Books depicting future occurrences

Procedure: 1. During play, model target future-tense verb forms. You could also use situation photos depicting something that will happen. Use familiar activities, such as a birthday party—most children know the birthday-party sequence:

Someone will light the candles on the birthday cake.

Everyone will sing happy birthday.

The birthday child will blow out the candles.

The birthday child will open presents.

Another highly familiar situation is going through the drive-through at a fast-food restaurant. Here is a likely sequence:

Mom will drive up to the speaker.

She will say what they want to eat.

She will drive to the window and pick up the food.

2. Give special vocal emphasis to the words *will* or *going to* when prompting. What **will** she do? What is **going to** happen?

Tips for Children with Type 2 or Type 3 ELD

• With children who have Type 2 or Type 3 ELD, it is best to use situations and vocabulary that are familiar, very meaningful, and relevant to the child. It can be positive or negative, such as "Tomorrow my grandparents will come," or "I broke that glass; my dad will be mad."

• Use situations that have sensorimotor components, such as putting toys away.

• Use visual cues, gestures, symbols, or words to cue future-tense production as needed.

- Sequential thinking is very difficult for many children with Type 2 or Type 3 ELD. You must probe to determine that the child understands the concept of future tense and is not just repeating the verb form embedded in the prompt. Probes using inferences are helpful, such as this one:

  Prompt: Look out, Pooh!

  Target Response: He is going to fall.

- See Activity 14, pages 141-142, for further suggestions for using inferences.

Treatment Stage 4: Activity 3

Skill: The child produces early-developing sentences with correct noun-verb agreement.

Description: The child produces sentences with subject-verb agreement (i.e., a singular noun form with a singular verb form and a plural noun form with plural verb form).

Materials: Props and toy characters for symbolic play

Two sets of action photos, a single-subject set and a multiple-subject set

Books showing single subjects and groups engaged in activities

Procedure:
1. During play or when using action photos or reading a book, model correct production of subject-verb agreement. Be sure to use vocabulary that is familiar to the child and that is of high interest.

2. Pause and wait with anticipation for the child to produce a sentence with subject-verb agreement.

3. If the child does not produce the target utterance, prompt with questions such as "What is Danny doing?"

4. If the child does not produce the target response, model and prompt for imitation.

Tips for Children with Type 2 or Type 3 ELD

- Sometimes using a cloze procedure ("fill in the blank") is helpful before requiring the child to produce a whole sentence. For example, you could say "What does the duck do? The duck ____. What do the ducks do? The ducks ____."

- If the children with Type 2 or Type 3 ELD have reading skills, they could use sentence strips as visual cues.

Skill: The child uses pronouns correctly.

Description: The child will use singular and plural pronouns in sentences, including these two levels:

> **Level 1**   he, him, his, she, her, you, your
>
> **Level 2**   it, we, us, our, ours, they, them, their, these, those

Materials: Props and toy characters for symbolic play

Two sets of action photos, a single-subject set and a multiple-subject set

Books depicting people doing activities

Procedure: 1. During play or other activity, model the correct production of early-developing (Level 1) pronouns. Be sure to use vocabulary and concepts familiar to the child.

2. Pause and wait with anticipation for the child to produce a sentence with a correct pronoun.

3. If the child does not produce a correct sentence response, model again and prompt the child to imitate.

Tips for Children with Type 2 or Type 3 ELD

- Visual cues often help children with Type 2 or Type 3 ELD. For example, you could teach *his* and *her* with paper dolls and a set of paper clothing that had to go with each one. A frilly dress, hair ribbons, and a purse would belong to *her.*

- Children with Type 2 or Type 3 ELD children often "memorize" responses after a single presentation of the stimulus. If that happens, change the training photos often. One source of inexpensive photos is the family-oriented magazines available at grocery store checkout counters.

- Text cues and sentence strips might also be useful. Sometimes color-coding specific gender pronouns can be helpful. Mail-order catalogs are good sources of photos.

- Matching games can be helpful. Match gender-specific words to the appropriate pronoun, such as matching *mom, girl, grandma,* and *lady* with *she.*

Treatment Stage 4: Activity 5

Skill: The child uses early developing *Wh-* questions.

Description: The child will use early-developing *Wh-* questions, including *who, what, where, how much,* and *when*.

Materials: Photos of people familiar to the child

Materials needed for familiar activities, such as the following:

    crayons and paper for coloring
    dishes and utensils for eating
    toothbrush and toothpaste for brushing teeth
    table and chair
    clay or craft dough

Procedure:

1. Set up situations for appropriate question production. Here are some examples:

   Before the session, hide an item or items needed to participate in a favorite, familiar activity. Attempt the activity without the needed items and model "Oh, no! **Where** is the _____?"

   Place a stack of photos of familiar and favorite people face-down. Model "**Who** is it?" and try to guess who the person in the photo will be when you turn it faceup.

   Make some sort of figure with modeling clay or dough and wonder out loud "**What** is it?" Then indicate what it is and point out its parts. "Oh, it's a face. Look, here are the eyes and the nose."

2. Pause and wait with anticipation for the child to produce a *Wh-* question.

3. If the child does not produce a correct sentence response, model again and prompt the child to imitate.

4. Remember to get multiple productions of target question forms.

- Use visual cues and gestures as much as possible. If the child can read, you may want to have a chart to cue through word association.

place = where

person = who

thing or object = what

- Sometimes it is helpful to make up question association games. Write questions in one color and answers in a different color, such as this set:

Who is it?

It is David.

Skill: The child identifies (a) object features and functions and (b) objects by feature and function.

Description: The child identifies an object by features or function, and the child identifies an object when given a description including features and function of the object.

Materials: A variety of familiar common objects
Photos or pictures of familiar common objects

Procedure:
1. In a game context, such as a "Scavenger Hunt," ask the child to find and label all items with a particular attribute, such as everything that's soft. Also in a game context, ask the child to find and label all the items that have a given function, such as things you use to draw. You can do this same activity with photos or picture cards instead of actual objects.

2. Play a guessing game. Present a description of an object as a riddle, such as "I'm thinking of something that . . . ." or "What has a beak and two wings?"

3. If the child is confused, present the prompt again, and ask the child to think about what it might be. Then present the next cue, and eliminate possibilities. Go through the clues, and help the child eliminate possibilities until you come to the target item. Review all the clues together to "make sure we are right."

Tips for Children with Type 2 or Type 3 ELD

- Children with Type 2 and Type 3 ELD need many examples to really understand a concept. Often what they learn is so specific to a certain item or small set of items that it doesn't generalize to other items. Offer many, many examples.

- Some children with Type 2 ELD and many with Type 3 ELD have difficulty with reversing their thinking. If you name an item, they can give you the features or function of that item without difficulty. If you name the features or function of the item first and then ask for the name of it, these children often have difficulty. Be sure to practice both of these tasks until they are mastered.

Treatment Stage 4: Activity 7

Skill: The child describes part-whole relationships.

Description: The child will identify the parts of an item or, when given the parts, will be able to identify the whole item.

Materials: Common objects
Photos or pictures of familiar common objects
Toys

Procedure:

1. Looking at toys or photos, label each part of the item. Make sure the child touches each part as she repeats the label. You may also incorporate part/whole activities into drawing activities. Draw the parts of a car, a house, a person, a flower, a tree, a bike, an animal, etc.

2. Ask the child to label the parts as you point to each part of an object. Model the correct response if the child responds incorrectly or appears not to know the name of a part.

3. When the child demonstrates proficiency with labeling parts of items, reverse the process. In the context of a guessing game or a hidden object, list the parts of an item, and ask the child to guess the object. During the drawing activities, draw an item and tell the child the parts you are drawing. Have the child positioned so she cannot see it. When you have completed the drawing, ask if the child can guess what you drew.

4. If the child has difficulty or can't recall a specific label (part or whole), present the prompt again, and cue or model the correct response as needed.

Tips for Children with Type 2 or Type 3 ELD

- Some children with Type 2 ELD and many with Type 3 ELD have difficulty with part/ whole relationships, such as identifying handles on items, particularly if the child has motor-planning deficits. Remember that if a child can't figure what she is supposed to do with a part motorically, chances are she will have some difficulty learning what the part is and what it does.

- Try to work on items in sets that have features in common. For example, work first on the parts of a car and then on the parts of a house—both have doors and windows. Alternatively, work first on people and then on animals—both have ears, eyes, noses, mouths, and legs.

Skill: The child indicates negation.

Description: The child indicates *not, can't* or *don't* in reference to object features, including color *(not red)*, shape *(not a square)*, size *(not small)*, texture *(not rough)*, or function *(what we don't/can't eat)*.

Materials: A variety of common objects, including several from the same category of objects, such as toy trucks, cars, and tractors

Photos of common objects

Procedure:
1. Present objects that, except for one, are all from the same category, have a feature in common, or have the same function.

2. Prompt the child to tell you which one does not belong or is different from the others.

3. If the child appears confused and does not respond or responds incorrectly, prompt again and model the correct answer, pointing out how the target item differs from the group.

Tips for Children with Type 2 or Type 3 ELD

- Often children with Type 2 or Type 3 ELD have tremendous difficulty comprehending the presence of one attribute and the absence of an attribute for the same item, such as *The sock is red but not striped.*

- Sometimes it helps to use a visual cue, such as a red or black **X** over an illustration of an object, attribute, or action to indicate *not, can't,* or *don't*, as on a no-parking sign. Below is an example showing *something you don't eat.*

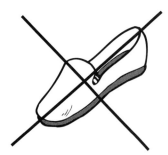 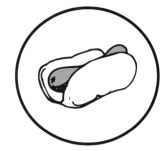

Treatment Stage 4: Activity 9

Skill: The child uses comparative and superlative descriptors.

Description: The child describes attribute differences between two objects, people, or animals using comparative *(-er)* descriptors and among three or more objects, people, or animals using superlative *(-est)* descriptors.

Materials: Props of the same thing in different sizes, such as 4 toy dogs or 4 toy trucks, 4 balls, 4 dolls, etc.

Paper, scissors, and glue

Procedure:

1. Present a very small dog followed by a big dog, a bigger dog, and the biggest dog. Alternatively, you could use paper dolls or dolls.

2. Ask the child to find the correct ball for each dog—the little ball for the small dog, the big ball for the big dog, the bigger ball for the bigger dog, and the biggest ball for the biggest dog.

3. If the child has difficulty, present the prompt again, and model and cue as necessary.

4. Repeat this activity using other descriptors, such as *long-longer-longest, short-shorter-shortest,* etc.

Tips for Children with Type 2 or Type 3 ELD

- Be sure to use familiar vocabulary and props. Even at this stage in language development, motor planning and coordination can be a problem.

- Make the activities problem-solving in nature, but fun, such as "This doll has bigger feet, so she needs bigger shoes."

- Be sure the child masters the comparative *(-er)* form before introducing the *-est* superlative form.

Skill: The child identifies object composition.

Description: The child identifies the basic component materials of objects, including paper, glass, metal, wood, plastic, cloth, and leather.

Materials: Familiar items made of wood, plastic, glass[1], paper, fabric, leather, and metal

Items made of a combination of materials, such as eyeglasses with metal frames

Procedure:
1. Present several objects. Later, present photos of objects.

2. Prompt the child to identify the material each object is made of.

3. If the child is confused or responds incorrectly, repeat the prompts, and cue and model the correct answer as necessary.

4. Present several examples of a particular material if child continues to answer incorrectly.

Tips for Children with Type 2 or Type 3 ELD

• Some children with Type 2 ELD and many with Type 3 ELD often have tremendous difficulty with identifying object composition. Sometimes they have difficulty viewing an object as having multiple classifications, such as "It is wood, and it is a table." They do not see the need to know what something is made of—if it's a table, it's a table. To make this task relevant for these children, put the need to know the composition of something into a problem-solving context. For example, if you are going to clean a window and a table, you have to use cleaners designed for each one.[2] If you use furniture polish on a mirror, it will smear. If you use glass cleaner on a wooden table, the cleaner will stain the table.

• You could also show pictures of how things made of wood or glass are made. Trees from the forest go to the mill and then to the furniture factory, where the table is made.

---

[1] School or facility rules and risk-management policies may prohibit the use of glass on-site with children. Be sure to check. Windows, computer screens, and bathroom mirrors are good alternate sources for glass objects.

[2] School or facility rules and risk-management policies may prohibit the use of cleaners around children. Often secondary vocational-education programs do permit the use of such cleaners by or around children.

Treatment Stage 4: Activity 11

Skill:	The child compares and contrasts objects.
Description:	The child tells how two objects are alike and how they are different.
Materials:	Familiar objects that have a common characteristic, such as being round, the same color, the same shape, the same texture, the same composition, or having the same function.
Procedure:	1. Present two objects to the child, and ask him to tell you how the items are alike, such as "They are both ____" or "They both have ____."
	2. If the child gives an incorrect response, repeat the prompt, and model the correct response, asking the child to repeat it.
	3. Then ask the child to state how the items are different, such as "One has/is ____, but the other has/is ____."
	4. If the child does not respond or produces an incorrect response, model the correct response for the child to repeat.

Tips for Children with Type 2 or Type 3 ELD

• Often children with Type 2 or Type 3 ELD have difficulty seeing how items can be alike and different at the same time. They may need reminders that things can be alike in some ways and be different in others at the same time.

• Children with Type 2 or Type 3 ELD who can read often benefit from charts, such as the one on the following page. Here are some example target responses using the information from the chart:

"They are both _____."

"But they are made of different materials. One is made of _____. The other is made of _____."

"They are used in different ways. You play with a Frisbee, and you put food on a plate."

Comparison Chart

	Object 1 **red Frisbee**	Object 2 **red plate**
Color →	red	red
Shape →	round	round
Size →	9 inches	11 inches
Texture →	smooth	smooth
Made Of →	plastic	paper
Function →	throw it, play with it	put food on it

Treatment Stage 4: Activity 12

Skill: The child identifies *real* and *pretend*.

Description: The child identifies what is real and can really happen versus what is made-up or fantasy.

Materials: Pictures from a children's book or a movie depicting fantasy
Pictures of people doing "real life" things

Procedure:
1. Present fantasy pictures and ask, "Could we REALLY do this?" Use familiar situations and experiences.

2. If the child seems confused or gives an incorrect response, prompt again, and model the answer, explaining the difference between reality and fantasy.

Tips for Children with Type 2 or Type 3 ELD

• *Pretend* or *fantasy* and *real* are difficult concepts for many children with Type 2 ELD and most children with Type 3 ELD. Present meaningful situations that are very familiar. For example, present Peter Pan learning to fly. Point out that people can't fly like birds. We can only fly in planes. People flying like birds is fantasy.

Another good fantasy example from *Alice in Wonderland* is Alice shrinking after eating magic mushrooms. People don't shrink and grow like that in real life.

Talking animals is also a good example of fantasy, particularly if the child has a pet. Point out that dogs can't talk in real life, but they do in movies, cartoons, and even sometimes in books.

• Before working on *real* and *fantasy* directly, preteach by labeling experiences as *real* or *fantasy*. This preteaching will get the child used to thinking about the concepts and the vocabulary.

139

Skill:	The child identifies absurdities (silly things).
Description:	The child identifies absurdities, such as eating with a shoe, writing with a banana, or wearing shoes that are too big or too small.
Materials:	Props for enacting silly situations, such as eating with a shoe Photos or illustrations depicting absurdities
Procedure:	1. During play, pretend to eat a shoe or put a hat on your foot, or try to put the child's shoe or your foot, announcing you are "soooo silly." 2. Prompt the child to tell what is silly. If she responds correctly, prompt her to explain why it is silly. 3. If the child is confused or responds incorrectly, prompt again, and model the correct response. Explain why it is silly. 4. Later, present pictures showing absurdities. Ask the child to tell what is so silly.

Tips for Children with Type 2 or Type 3 ELD

• Use very familiar objects and props.

• Really dramatize the absurdity. Try very hard to put that baby shoe on your BIG FOOT.

• Use concepts with a strong sensorimotor component. For example, show someone wearing a swimsuit in the snow or a snow suit at the beach. Children should be able to relate to *very hot* (sweating, thirsty) and *very cold* (shaking, saying "Brr!").

Treatment Stage 4: Activity 14

Skill: The child responds to inferences.

Description: The child produces actions, words, phrases, or sentences in response to inferences.

Materials: Action figures or baby dolls

Props for eating, sleeping, and other familiar activities (If possible, place props on the side of the child away from you so the child has to respond to your inferences to keep the play going because you can't reach the prop or props.)

Procedure:
1. During play with action figures or baby dolls, pretend to be a doll or a character and say "I'm soooooo hungry!"

2. Pause to see if the child will give you food and/or make a verbal reference to food. For example, the child might reach for toy food and pretend to feed the action figure or the doll. The child might make a verbal reference to the food, such as "Here is a _____" or "Eat _____."

3. If the child doesn't respond, repeat the inference, and pair it with a direct request and a gesture toward the food. As a character, prompt with "I'm sooo hungry! Please give me some food!" Reach dramatically for the food, which should be positioned out of your reach but near the child.)

4. Over time, fade the use of the direct statement paired with the inference so that the child learns to respond to the inference alone. Here are some other inference situations you could use:

   Prompt: So tired! (Put the baby to bed.)

   Prompt: I don't want to play ball anymore. (Inference: Let's play something else.)

Tips for Children with Type 2 or Type 3 ELD

- Indirect statements are particularly difficult for children with Type 2 or 3 ELD. Language is very literal for them. If the children can read or understand math concepts, you could use a graphic representation of a language equation:

I am so hungry. = I want to eat.

I am so tired. = I want to rest.

- Be sure to use very familiar, relevant situations and vocabulary. Situations that are usually interesting include the following:

    Prompt: Oh, no, it's broken! (Inference: Let's try to fix it or find another one.)

    Prompt: We're going to (name an activity or task), and I can't find the _____. (Inference: Where is/are the missing item/s needed to do the activity?)

Skill: The child produces a detailed description.

Description: The child produces a detailed description of a single-subject scene and then a situation scene, including what is happening, where it is happening (location—*kitchen* and position—*on the floor*), who is doing it, and when it happened, including relevant information about affect, color, sizes, shapes, patterns, and other attributes.

Materials: Single-subject photo cards and a barrier

      Situation photos or illustrations and a barrier

      A Viewmaster and disks

      Picture sequence card sets are good for this activity. For example, the child describes a scene and you have to identify which of the four cards he is talking about. You will need duplicate sets, one set for you and a set from which the child can select one to describe.

Procedure: 1. Position a single-subject photo so that you cannot see it. Tell the child you are going to play a guessing game. The child is going to describe the picture you can't see; you're going to guess what it is.

      2. Place three pictures in front of you that have many of the same visual elements.

      3. Ask the child to describe his target card so you can guess it. The child should be able to tell you information such as the following:

         Who is pictured?

         What is going on/happened?

         Where is it?

         Gender of the character

         Age

         Clothing

         Color, shape, or texture of hair

      4. If the child is confused or responds incorrectly, prompt again as necessary. Give cues, and model the correct response as needed.

Tips for Children with Type 2 or Type 3 ELD

- Sometimes Children with Type 2 or Type 3 ELD who can read benefit from a script where they fill in the blanks, such as "I see a cat. He is on/in/at _____. He is wearing _____. He looks like he is _____ years old. He is holding a _____." Later they can generate sentences to describe things independently.

- Often children with Type 2 or Type 3 ELD need a lot of assistance with this activity. At first, you and the child may have to develop the descriptions together.

The Importance of Visualization

"Words change to pictures in your mind and those pictures change back to words to help you verbalize."

—Bell (1991)

Children need to be able to visualize or see a picture when they hear words and sentences. Visualization allows children to recall experiences, predict outcomes, problem-solve, and think sequentially.

Being able to describe what one sees is an important skill. Children first learn the words to describe what they see. When they hear the words later, they can picture what they have heard.

Treatment Stage 4: Activity 16

Skill: The child directs the action of others.

Description: The child gives directions to others during cleanup and during games, such as "Simon Says."

Materials: Toys
Materials for tabletop activities

Procedure:

1. When it is time to clean up, ask the child to direct the other children in what to do. Alternatively, play "Simon Says" and have the child be Simon, directing the other children.

2. If child has difficulty or gives incorrect directions, prompt again, and cue and/or model the target responses as needed.

Tips for Children with Type 2 or Type 3 ELD

- Sometimes children with Type 2 or Type 3 ELD have difficulty switching roles. They can follow directions, but they don't always know how to switch roles and give directions. Sometimes a visual prop helps the role switch. For example, a toy microphone or megaphone may cue who is giving directions.

- For "Simon Says," designate a "Simon Spot." Whoever stands in the "Simon Spot" is Simon and gives directions for the game.

Treatment Stage 4: Activity 17

Skill: The child plays simple games.

Description: The child sets up a game, takes turns, states the object of the game, recognizes when the game is over, and states the winner of the game.

Materials: Simple board games, such as "Candyland," "Memory," "Lotto" and "Connect Four"

Simple card games, such as "Fish"

Simple action games, such as "Tag" and "A Tisket, a Tasket"

Simple paper-pencil games, such as "Tic-Tac-Toe" and "Hangman"

Procedure:
1. Give the prompt "Let's play _____."

2. Prompt the child to set up the game. Provide assistance as necessary.

3. Ask the child if he remembers how to play. Ask him to tell you how to determine who goes first.

4. Prompt the child to take a turn. Provide assistance as needed.

5. Play until the game ends. Wait to see if the child recognizes when the game is over. Cue him, if necessary.

6. Prompt to see if the child recognizes and states the winner.

7. Prompt the child to explain how the winner won. For example, "You/I got the most cards" or "You/I covered all the squares on your/my lotto card first."

Tips for Children with Type 2 or Type 3 ELD

- Children with Type 2 or Type 3 ELD often have difficulty "reversing the process" or reversing roles. Help them learn that sometimes they have to answer, and sometimes they have to ask. Use visual cues or cue cards to help let them know what role they are playing.

- Children with Type 2 or Type 3 ELD also sometimes have difficulty when they have to predict outcomes and make judgments about the "best moves" to make in a game. They don't prompt themselves to predict consequences by thinking "If I do this, then you will do this." Having kids verbalize "what might happen" will help them in the decision-making process.

- Sometime it helps to use the Lotto cards and Memory cards in labeling activities early in the language-learning process. When you reintroduce the materials in a game context, the children should have an easier time, and they'll learn multiple uses for things.

Treatment Stage 4: Activity 18

Skill:　　　　The child takes turns in conversation.

Description:　　The child takes several turns in conversational exchanges.

Materials:　　Situation pictures to discuss
Something broken to problem-solve about
Book
Brief videotape

Procedure:　　1. Ask a question or make a statement to the child that requires a response. Be sure to make your stimulus sentences meaningful to the child. Use concepts and vocabulary the child is familiar with, and discuss topics that are of interest to her.

2. Pause and signal anticipation of a response. If necessary, provide visual cues, and repeat the prompt.

3. Sometimes using a device with a microphone to pass back and forth helps a child know how and when to take a turn in a conversation.

4. If the child does not respond or responds incorrectly, model and prompt for imitation.

Tips for Children with Type 2 or Type 3 ELD

- You could practice conversational turn-taking by building a conversation script. Use one sentence strip per sentence/turn. Write the responses for each speaker in a different color.

- Children with Type 2 or 3 ELD can become very skilled at answering direct questions. Responding to inferences is much more difficult. For further information about ways to teach inferences, see Activity 14 on pages 141-142.

Treatment Stage 4: Activity 19

Skill: The child stays on topic during conversations.

Description: The child maintains a topic for several conversational exchanges.

Materials: No specific materials

Procedure:

1. Start a conversation about a familiar, high-interest topic about which the child knows a lot.

2. Make a statement that requires a response. You may want to embed the response in the question or statement, such as the following:

Clinician:	I think I want more candy.
Child:	I want more candy, too.
Clinician:	What kind should we have? I really like jelly beans.
Child:	Jelly beans are good.
Clinician:	My favorite jelly beans are the green ones.

3. If the child veers off topic, let him know. For example, "I said '_____', and then you said '_____'. I am confused."

Tips for Children with Type 2 or Type 3 ELD

- Practice identifying statements that are associated and not associated.

- If the child can read, practice identifying sentences that are and are not related to a particular topic.

- If the child can read, give the child a script of a conversation. Enact the conversation together.

- Identify ways to respond to sentence types. For example, if someone says "I like _____," you could respond "I like _____, too" or "I don't like _____." Sometimes making a chart or a "tree" to show the types of statements or questions and their possible responses is helpful.

- Children with Type 2 or 3 ELD often do fine with topic management if the topic is about familiar, concrete things they can see and hold. When the topic steers to emotions or abstract concepts, such as *bravery* or *pride*, these children often have more difficulty. These children will require a lot of meaningful examples for abstract concepts in order to understand them.

- To add visual cues, you could have a photo of a place, situation, or activity attached to a sheet of paper. Draw a chart on the paper, and label sections for "Related" and "Not Related" statements. If the child makes a statement that is on topic or related to a current conversation, make a green check or a green happy face in the "Related" section. If the child is off the topic, make a red check or a red sad face in the "Not Related" section. Here is an example:

Topic: **At the Playground Today**

Related ☺	Not Related ☹

Treatment Stage 4: Activity 20

Skill: The child repairs conversational mistakes.

Description: The child engages in appropriate conversational repair when the listener appears to have misunderstood what was said.

Materials: No specific materials

Procedure:
1. While engaged in a conversation with the child, pretend not to understand what the child has said.

2. Make comments or perform actions based on the misunderstood communication. Do literally what the child said.

3. When the child looks confused, say "Didn't you say _____?"

4. When the child corrects her mistake, be sure to thank the child because you were "so confused." If the child cannot give a logical and/or a grammatical restatement of the original information, model for the child: "Oh, you said _____."

Tips for Children with Type 2 or Type 3 ELD

- Make sure the "misunderstood message" has a strong visual cue to indicate that the information was misunderstood. For example, if the child has asked for an orange, give her an apple. When she looks confused or protests, tell her you misunderstood. Tell her to ask for what she wants again.

- Make sure when you rehearse handling misunderstood messages that the vocabulary and concepts are very familiar to the child.

Treatment Stage 4: Activity 21

Skill: The child relates experiences.

Description: The child relates experiences in simple narratives of three or more sentences.

Materials: Photos
       Finished art projects
       Finished cooking projects

Procedure: 1. Select and mention a recent, special experience of the child's.

       2. Prompt the child to tell you about it.

       3. Prompt the child with specific questions, if necessary.

       4. Sometimes ask the child to dictate the narrative to you so that you can make a little book about it.

Tips for Children with Type 2 or Type 3 ELD

- Be sure to use very familiar vocabulary and themes.

- Provide visual cues, such as a schedule. If the child was engaged in a project, you could use the finished product as a visual cue, such as an art project or a cooking activity.

- You might be able to use "backward chaining." You start by saying the first two sentences, and the child has to say the third. Subsequently, the child gives the last two sentences, and then gives three or more sentences about the earlier part of the experience.

Treatment Stage 4: Activity 22

Skill: The child retells a story.

Description: The child retells or dictates a story read to him, using three or more logically-sequenced sentences forming a simple narrative.

Materials: Storybooks
Props associated with the storybooks

Procedure:
1. Read or tell a story with a prop or props.

2. Encourage the child to retell the story. Use props if additional cueing is needed.

3. If the child has difficulty, model the first sentence, and encourage the child to continue the story.

4. If the child still has difficulty, use cloze sentences (fill-in-the-blank) along with visual cues or props.

Tips for Children with Type 2 or Type 3 ELD

- Use familiar vocabulary and themes.

- Make sure the stories selected have strong visual representation of the story action.

- Have the child use visual props or actions to cue recall of the story.

- If the child can read, make sentence strips, and ask the child to retell the story using the sentence strips.

Treatment Stage 4: Activity 23

Skill: The child produces a simple explanation.

Description: The child will produce a simple explanation of how to do something or how to make something.

Materials: Materials for specific activities

Procedure: 1. Do a simple activity, such as a food preparation, an art activity, or a simple game.

   2. Ask the child to explain to another child how to do the activity, or tell the child you need to write down the directions for a particular game or project so that you can give them to another child, and you need help. Ask the child to dictate his explanation to you.

Tips for Children with Type 2 or Type 3 ELD

• If the child can read, as you and the child complete each step of an activity, write what you did on sentence strips, numbering each strip. If the child can't read, use picture symbols or simple drawing. When you're finished, you'll have a set of directions to use as visual cues.

• Make sure that what you ask the child to describe is very meaningful to the child and has a strong sensorimotor component and strong visual cues.

Treatment Stage 4: Activity 24

Skill: The child predicts outcomes.

Description: The child predicts outcomes of simple stories, predicts who or what he will see at a particular place, and predicts what will happen if _____.

Materials: Situation photo cards or pictures

Storybooks with a simple theme that builds to a single, familiar outcome and that has a strong sensorimotor component, such as the following:

> Children are jumping on a bicycle.
>
> They are riding very fast.
>
> They see a stop sign, but they can't stop.
>
> They see a red light, but they can't stop.
>
> They are going faster and faster, and they can't stop.
>
> Oh, no! Oh, no! What is going to happen?
>
> They are going to _____. (crash)

Procedure:
1. Read part of a story or show some photo cards.

2. Ask the child to predict what might happen.

3. If the child seems confused or gives an incorrect response, reread the story or present the stimulus photo again.

4. Prompt the child to predict, then cue or model the correct response as necessary.

Tips for Children with Type 2 or Type 3 ELD

- Use very familiar concepts with strong sensorimotor components. Crashes and broken items seem to be easier for children to remember than other stories.

- Provide visual cues and movement cues as necessary. Act it out with the child as necessary, or act it out with props and commercial toy characters.

Skill: The child tells a brief story.

Description: The child tells a brief story of two or more sentences that may include information about the story's characters, setting, and plot.

Materials: Props and commercial toy characters
Writing utensils and paper

Procedure: 1. Prompt the child by saying, "Let's make up a story about _____."
Use props and commercial toy characters or draw the story.

2. The child states two or more related sentences about an action related to a character or characters.

3. If the child has difficulty, assist by prompting with cloze (fill-in-the-blank) sentences.

4. The stories should include action, emotions, and problem-solving. Cue and model as necessary to help the child elicit these story elements.

Tips for Children with Type 2 or Type 3 ELD

• Be sure to use very familiar vocabulary and themes.

• Sometimes providing visual cues, such as numbered boxes, helps the child to tell more. Use one sentence or idea for each box.

Treatment Stage 4: Activity 26

Skill: The child verbally problem-solves.

Description: The child suggests solutions to a simple, familiar problem, such as *You drop your spoon on the floor; what should you do?*

Materials: Situation photos
"Sabotaged" toys or materials

Procedure:
1. During play or when attempting an activity with a sabotaged toy, point out a problem to the child.

2. Prompt the child by asking "What should we do?"

3. Pause for the child to make some suggestions.

4. If the child has difficulty, prompt again. As needed, cue and model the correct responses.

Tips for Children with Type 2 or Type 3 ELD

• Children with Type 2 or Type 3 ELD may need to be offered several choices of ways to solve a given problem.

• Use familiar, meaningful examples first. For example, the child attempts to draw with a marker that is dry and must problem-solve what to do.

Chapter 8

Understanding Challenging Behavior

Children who have communication problems, especially expressive language delay (ELD), often exhibit challenging behavior. For all children, especially children with ELD, challenging behavior is often a form of communication. To understand and manage challenging behavior in children, SLPs must ask and answer the right questions. But just knowing the answers to these questions does not really help if you don't do anything useful with the information. This chapter will suggest questions to ask to get the information you need and suggest some basic strategies for using the information to manage challenging behavior.

Why is it important for SLPs to understand and address challenging behavior?

SLPs can be more productive in therapy with any and all patients if they are skilled in handling challenging behavior. SLPs should spend therapy time doing therapy, not managing behavior. SLPs who attempt to manage behavior without a basic knowledge of behavioral principles sometimes do things to "handle" behavior that actually reinforce and increase the frequency of the behavior rather than decreasing it.

If the challenging behavior serves a purpose for the child that can be communicated more appropriately with conventional communication, the SLP is, in many instances, the best person on the child's team to determine what type of communication that child should substitute for the challenging behavior.

In the educational setting, with the reauthorization of federal mandatory special education legislation (IDEA, 1997), if the child presents with behavior that makes effective implementation of his individual educational program (IEP) difficult, then a behavioral plan must be developed. SLPs are better able to participate more fully in the development and implementation of such plans if they have some basic knowledge about the principles of behavioral intervention.

Finally, professionals who work directly with children with communication deficits and developmental deficits will be happier and more enthusiastic and avoid "burnout" if they can manage the behavior effectively instead of the behavior managing them.

What are the specific behaviors you and others are trying to manage?

If we say a child is "having a bad day," that doesn't give specific information about the child's behavior. If, on the other hand, we say "Every time I start to work on X, he starts to throw the therapy materials," then we have enough specific information to begin to do a functional analysis of behavior. Here are the questions we need to answer:

> What does the child do?
>
> How long does it last?
>
> How intense is it?
>
> How often does it occur?

We need to be able to describe the challenging behavior and collect some data about it. We need to look at frequency (how often it happens), duration (how long it lasts), intensity, as well as where and with whom the behavior occurs. These are the kinds of questions that are answered when we do a functional analysis of behavior.

Would the behavior be appropriate in another environment?

We see examples of this phenomena frequently. We often tell children "Remember to use your inside voice." In other words, a loud voice is appropriate in some places and at some times, but not at others. Children would then have to be taught that louder voices are for outside.

What impact is the behavior having on treatment?

Does the behavior interfere with the acquisition of new skills or the performance of skills the child has already learned?

Does this behavior stall the child's progress or cause him to regress?

Does the behavior interfere with classroom or therapy procedures?

Is it disruptive to the entire group, and does it make it difficult to meet therapy goals?

We need to look at the behavior and determine if it is really impacting therapy or if it is just very annoying. We have to prioritize which behaviors we need to address first. Those behaviors that are dangerous, if observed in therapy, must be addressed first. If, for example, you have a child who likes to run away, decreasing the frequency of running should be a high priority.

Examine the child's behavior and its effect on other children. Throwing things or tipping furniture can be dangerous to other children; laughing inappropriately is annoying but not dangerous.

Look at how the child's behavior is effecting his skill performance or rate of acquisition of new skills. For example, if a child is self-stimulating, it will be difficult for him to learn some functional play skills.

Something to Think About

If you are spending time reprimanding or punishing a child, he is not learning. Some therapists think that because a child is difficult to manage, it is okay if he does not make progress in therapy. The truth is, it's up to us to manage the child's behavior. The child is, after all, just that—a child. We are the professionals. It is our job to treat him and manage his behavior. It is not our job to accept less than optimal skill acquisition due to challenging behavior!

Why is the child exhibiting the behavior? What purpose does it serve?

In recent years, behaviorists have begun to look more closely at what motivates challenging behavior. Why do children do what they do? Children engage in challenging behavior for one or more of four purposes: avoidance, access, attention, or for sensory input.

Avoidance	Challenging behavior occurs to reduce the demand or aversiveness of a situation. Some children engage in inappropriate behavior to get out of doing something they don't want to do.
Access	Challenging behavior occurs to gain access to preferred items or activities. Some children throw a tantrum to get a favorite toy or activity.
Attention	Challenging behavior occurs to gain social attention, such as a hug or a reprimand. Children often engage in challenging behavior to get attention from teachers or caregivers.
Sensory Input	Children sometimes engage in challenging behavior just because it feels good. Children may spin around because it feels good to spin around. The notion of *feels good* bears some explanation. For children with sensory-system problems, *feel good* is the alternative to feeling awful rather than the alternative to a neutral state. Swinging, spinning, or some other active motor behavior may help some children handle and process stimuli more comfortably.

Does something in the environment contribute to the increase or decrease of the behavior?

Setting events are environmental contexts that may contribute to the increase or decrease of the child's behavior. Sometimes just modifying the environment is enough to eliminate a specific challenging behavior. The contexts usually examined when doing a functional analysis of behavior include biological contexts, social-cognitive contexts, and physical contexts.

Biological Contexts	The biological state of the child may contribute to the behavior. Assess the child's physical state. Is he tired, hungry, or sick? Does he have some difficulty hearing? Is he experiencing some sensorimotor problems?
Social-Cognitive Contexts	Some children have a difficult time if they don't get enough stimulation from the environment. Is there too much "down time" during transitions? Does the child have the skills to complete the task, or is he demonstrating challenging behavior because he's frustrated?
Physical Contexts	Think about the physical context. Is the room too hot, too cold, too noisy, too bright, too dark, and so forth? Some children do not appear to be bothered very much by the physical context. Others, especially those with sensory defensiveness, have a very difficult time in overstimulating environments.

What else should I know about challenging behavior?

How often does it occur?

When does it happen? What time of day does it occur?

Where is it most likely to happen?

With whom is it most likely to occur?

During which activity is it most likely to occur?

What actions or events seem to make the child happy and less likely to exhibit the challenging behavior?

Who makes the child happy? Who is least likely to be presented with the challenging behaviors?

Behavior specialists often conduct an ABC Assessment to understand problem behavior, as outlined in the box below.

ABC Behavior Assessment

A = **Antecedents**

Identify what happens before the behavior occurs.

What happened before the behavior occurred?

Did it trigger the behavior?

B = **Behavior**

Define the behavior.

C = **Consequences**

Describe what people do in response to the behavior.

What happens in response to the behavior?

Could this response to the behavior be reinforcing it?

Managing Challenging Behavior

After identifying and describing challenging behavior, identify some behavior-management strategies, and develop a plan. Often, challenging behavior is managed using the principles of Applied Behavior Analysis (ABA). Children with severely-challenging behavior may require the services of a behavioral psychologist or a certified behavior analyst. Don't hesitate to seek additional assistance addressing seriously-challenging behavior, including aggression or self-injurious behavior. Here are some ABA strategies that can be used with children who exhibit challenging behavior:

Extinction   Withholding reinforcement, usually by ignoring the behavior. This strategy is usually used in conjunction with differential reinforcement of other behavior.

Example: The child throws a tantrum to get what he wants. Ignore the tantrum and withhold attention until the child regains composure. Then attend to the child.

When to use it: Use it when you have determined that the behavior is attention-seeking behavior.

Positive Reinforcement	Events that will increase the probability that a certain behavior will recur. The actual items offered are reinforcers. Primary reinforcers are important to people because of our biology, such as foods or drinks. Secondary reinforcers are things we learn to like, such as toys, activities, or praise.
	Example: Give the child a ball when he uses the word *ball* to request it. Give him lots of praise for requesting the ball.
	When to use it: When you want to increase the frequency of a behavior. Positive reinforcement is only positive reinforcement if it increases the frequency of the behavior. Once a certain frequency has been reached, positive reinforcement may also be used to keep the behavior at the desired level.
Negative Reinforcement	Events that, when removed, increase the probability that a behavior will recur
	Example: If a child engages in inappropriate behavior and you appear disappointed, your reaction can sometimes function as a negative reinforcer. The child will engage in appropriate behavior so that you will be your pleasant self again and so that he can feel better.
	When to use it: Use it to increase the frequency of an appropriate response and decrease the frequency of an inappropriate behavior.
Punishment	A consequence that decreases the likelihood that a behavior will occur
	Example: A child does something he is not supposed to do and is firmly told "no."
	When to use it: When you want to decrease the frequency of a behavior.
Interval Schedule of Reinforcement	The delivery of reinforcers after a certain amount of time engaged in a target behavior you want to increase, or not engaging in a target behavior you want to decrease
	Example: The child gets a reward after five minutes of playing and interacting appropriately with peers. Conversely, the child is rewarded for not leaving his seat after a certain amount of time.

| | When to use it: | Use interval reinforcement when you want to increase the time a child stays with an activity or the length of time he can go without producing an inappropriate behavior you may be targeting. |

Ratio Schedule of Reinforcement

The delivery of reinforcers after a certain number of correct responses

| | Example: | The child gets a sticker after labeling ten action pictures correctly. |
| | When to use it: | Early on when you are trying to establish a behavior or skill, give reinforcement at a 1:1 ratio (one reinforcement for each correct response). Once the desired behavior has been established, adjust the rate of reinforcement so that the child must give you more responses to get the reinforcer. |

Differential Reinforcement of Other Behavior

Rewarding the child when he is doing an appropriate behavior. This strategy is often used in conjunction with extinction.

| | Example: | If the child likes to toss toys, reward him when he is playing appropriately with toys. |
| | When to use it: | Use it if the child exhibits behavior other than the inappropriate behavior. This strategy is particularly effective when used in conjunction with extinction. |

Time Out

The prompt and temporary removal of a child from an activity in response to inappropriate behavior. This strategy should not be used to eliminate avoidance behavior.

| | Example: | A child becomes aggressive within a group, so you remove her for a short period of time. |
| | When to use it: | Avoid using time out if you have determined the behavior is to avoid tasks. Behavior that is for gaining attention can often be managed with a time-out strategy. |

Shaping   Selectively reinforcing responses increasingly closer to a target behavior

Example: The child learns to say "Bah" to get bubbles. Then you require that he say "Bah-bah" to get the bubbles. Still later, you require "Bubbles" for him to get the bubbles.

When to use it: Sometimes children aren't ready to learn a whole skill, but they can learn small pieces and put them together.

Fading   Slowly removing prompts and cues to allow natural environmental stimuli to bring about the response

Example: Suppose the child needs the initial-sound cue /d/ to produce the word *dog* when he sees a picture of a dog. Later, you fade the initial-sound cue, and the child is still able to label pictures of dogs.

When to use it: As soon as the child shows proficiency.

The Extinction Burst

When implementing a plan to decrease behaviors, you may see a brief increase in the target behavior initially. Why? It's simple if you look at it from the child's point of view. The child engages in a particular behavior and gets a particular response. That behavior-response paradigm has become part of his life's routine. Then you implement a change. You don't respond to the behavior, or you respond in a different way. The child figures maybe you somehow missed the behavior, so he does it longer, stronger, and harder to get the response he wants. That's the "burst of behavior" before the frequency of the challenging behavior begins to decrease.

How do I know the behavior management is working?

Data Collection
Collect baseline data on the behavior that you have identified as being in need of management. Document how often it occurs (frequency). If appropriate, document how long it lasts (duration). If appropriate, document the intensity.

Implement a Strategy
Select a strategy or set of strategies to use. Start using them. Keep the team informed, and strive for consistency across the child's environments.

Monitor the Behavior
After a period of time, the frequency, duration, and intensity of the challenging behavior should decrease. Change takes time and may occur in small increments. Sometimes it is difficult to see improvements in behavior. Look for the following types of improvements when attempting to decrease inappropriate behavior:

Decrease in Frequency

The child engages in the behavior fewer times. For example, the child engages in temper tantrums four times a day on average instead of five. That's improvement!

Decrease in Duration

The child's temper tantrums only last approximately three minutes instead of ten minutes. That's improvement!

Decrease in Intensity

The child cries when he tantrums, but no longer throws himself onto the floor kicking and screaming. That's improvement!

Changing challenging behavior takes time, so stick with it!

Preventing Problem Behaviors

One of the best ways to handle problem behavior is to take steps in advance to prevent problem behavior. Here are some preventive measures:

- Understand basic ABA principles and their use.

- Arrange the therapy area to decrease the likelihood of problem behaviors.

- Identify the conditions that cause problem behavior, and change them or eliminate them, if possible.

- Know the child's skill levels to prevent boredom and frustration.

- Make sure problem or challenging behavior has consequences.

- Make sure tantrums don't pay.

- Know if the child is on medications and what the possible side effects are.

- Be consistent.

- Know if the child is following routine eating and sleeping patterns.

- Know the child's sensorimotor-processing profile.

- If the child needs predictability in his schedule, make sure to follow a schedule so the child can anticipate what is coming next.

- Let the child know in advance what is coming next to aid in transitions or to prepare for changes in the schedule.

- Provide visual supports, such as photos or picture-symbols, as needed.

- Make sure the child has opportunities to make choices.

- "Catch" the child being good. Be on the lookout for good behavior, and praise it right away when it happens.

- Use common sense. If a child likes to throw things, don't have anything throwable nearby. Especially early on, don't stack the deck against the child.

- Make up your mind today that you will not get into a power struggle with the child. Those are usually lose-lose situations.

- Remember that children are not bad. Sometimes what they **do** is challenging.

Perspective

When we think of managing behavior, we think of managing "challenging" behavior. I think we need to expand and expend:

> **Expand** our thinking to view the steps after the behavior is managed to be as important as the steps before.

> **Expend** as much energy motivating children to learn as we do managing the behavior that prevents them from learning.

Managing behavior is like a coin with **Management** on one side and **Motivation** on the other. Both sides of the coin are of equal value. Without both sides, the coin has little value.

But It Works!

I have a colleague who is an internationally-recognized behaviorist. Because of the kinds of children referred to me, our paths often cross.

I remember our first meeting. A parent informed me that I was going to be observed by a behavior specialist who was part of the child's treatment team. I had been working with this child for a few months. The behavior specialist wanted to observe the child across settings and with different individuals. I had had no difficulties with this particular child's behavior, although most did. I knew that I knew how to manage his behavior. In addition, the child was making remarkable gains in therapy, and it was generalizing to other settings. But I was nervous. What I was doing was not exactly ABA by the book as I had been taught.

- I did not always give specific praise, such as "Good (verb)-ing." Sometimes, I said "Awesome!"

- I often embedded commands, so the child was compliant on some level, but he didn't know it.

- Sometimes instead of punishment when the child was noncompliant, I redirected his attention. That might appear to some behaviorists as reinforcement of non-compliant behavior.

As the day approached, I was apprehensive. I knew I could defend my methods and strategies. I had enough data to show steady acquisition of skill and a steady decrease in the frequency of inappropriate and non-compliance behavior. I could prove that it was working. And yet . . . .

The appointed day arrived. The behavior "guru" observed, and I was determined to run my session as I always did and take the heat afterwards. When the session was over, I began our debriefing, not waiting for the behaviorist to begin what I knew would be an assault. I apologized for less-than-exemplary use of the principles of ABA and was prepared to plead my case. Before I could continue, he smiled and said, "Don't apologize for what you do. It works, doesn't it?"

Last Stop on the Road?

During the early part of my career, I was employed by a small suburban school district in the Midwest. We provided educational services for children with severe disabilities who resided at home and those who resided in nearby residential facilities. One housed individuals with developmental disabilities, and the other housed individuals with psychiatric disorders. Often children in educational programs in other school districts, programs for children with milder disabilities, would be moved "down" to our program. We were the last stop on the road.

The following two stories demonstrate what can happen with "last-stop" children if we use good management strategies.

Managing Behavior

Kenny came to our program with two full-time male aides and quite a reputation. I knew the reputation was probably true. I knew of Kenny from my days as a speech therapist at a nearby DD residential facility. Kenny could be sweet, but when he became angry, he threw tantrums. Big tantrums. Kenny was 6'6" and weighed about 280 lbs. I knew my colleagues had their work cut out for them. Kenny had been in an educable mentally-handicapped classroom in another school district. Even with two male aides, they could not control his behavior. Kenny was moved to our program because of our skill and expertise with students who exhibited challenging behavior.

Our staff was young, but well trained. Most of us were in our 20s and didn't have sense enough to know we were too young and inexperienced to successfully do what we did. For the most part, we saw challenging kids as something that made our jobs interesting, and we had fun in the process. Our job was to get the behavior managed, and manage it we did. By the end of the school year, Kenny was in a classroom for educable students. The classroom staff included a female teacher and a classroom aide. Two male "behavior aides" were out of a job!

Motivating Amy

Amy had been in another program for children with severe motor disabilities. She hadn't been successful in that environment, so she was moved to our district, which had programs for children who had severe mental retardation.

Amy was a beautiful child with big brown eyes. Her records indicated that she was severely retarded. I knew the staff at the school district she transferred from. They were very good; the reports of her skills were probably accurate. In addition to severe retardation, Amy also had severe cerebral palsy. She had very little head control and no extremity control. Her affect was generally flat, and she didn't respond to much. I learned later that Amy's family was from a culture that had a difficult time accepting disability.

At that time, our school district had a federally-funded project that looked at how children with severe disabilities learned in a specialized environment. The room was sensorimotor "happening." It had lights with dimmers, stereo music, ramps, swings, a waterbed, carpeted levels, and many cause-effect "experiences" built into the walls. I often worked with children in that room.

I had been working with Amy only a few weeks. One day, I carried her into the room and commented out loud, "Wow, it is dark in here." Her head swung around, and she look up at the light. Interesting.

Over the next several weeks, I found myself spending as much time as I could in Amy's classroom in addition to her regular therapy sessions. I explained to her teacher that I wanted to get a better handle on Amy's level of functioning. I usually ate my lunch quickly and spent at least half of my lunch period with Amy. The staff was happy to have me. All the children were severely physically and mentally handicapped, so they welcomed an extra pair of hands.

Amy was my charge for the period of time I was there. At first, she did not seem to be aware of me. Over time, she began to smile when I entered the room. Eventually, she would raise her head and smile. I

(continued on next page)

170

would spend time talking to her, teasing her. She would laugh. I knew she had more ability than anyone had seen before. I began my campaign on her behalf. I was due to go on maternity leave with my second child in a few months. I immediately transferred her to my colleague so that her treatment would be uninterrupted. I told my colleague that Amy was very smart, but we just hadn't seen it yet.

In June of that year, I moved out of state, but I kept in contact to keep tabs on Amy. She eventually left the program and went back to her old school district. She was placed in a program for children with physical disabilities. "Very smart indeed," they had told my colleague. "Normal intelligence," they thought.

Chapter 9

Language for a Life and a Lifetime

Language for a Life

Language occurs in the context of life. The context of life for young children with expressive language delay (ELD) is the home and the family. It may also be the preschool or day-care setting.

Communication with a child with ELD occurs within the context of relationships, such as relationships with parents and siblings or with day-care providers and preschool teachers. Therefore, we must try to understand as much as possible about the communication contexts for each child if our treatment is to be as effective as possible. We must make the communication skills we teach relevant and meaningful to the contexts that make up each young child's life—the relationships with his family and caregivers.

Make It Family-Friendly, Family-Focused

What we do for children with expressive language delay, we do for families of those children. When a child walks through the door for an evaluation and treatment, we ask many questions of the parents or caregivers. When did he walk? If he has any words, what are they, and when did he start using them? How many brothers or sisters does he have? How old are they? Are there pets in the family?

The answers to these and other questions are very important. Too often we fill in the blanks and move quickly and efficiently to the task of gathering information about language and communication skills. Perhaps instead of turning to the next page of the patient information form, we should pause briefly to get a mental picture of the child and his family. But this picture is not a posed family portrait. No, what we see in our minds should be more like a home video, complete with sound and action. Envision that child doing the things that children do in a family. See him playing, laughing, crying, requesting, refusing, teasing, and directing. See the child being curious, mischievous, jealous, confused, and affectionate. Store those images in your memory. Let them be the beacon that guides you and helps you design the most effective therapy.

Understanding Parents and the Grieving Process

Parents of children with significant disabilities often go through a grieving process as they come to terms with their children's disabilities. If we are to work effectively with these families, we need to have some understanding of the grieving process and recognize where parents may be in this process.

One of the most commonly-cited authors in this area is Elizabeth Kubler-Ross, author of *On Death and Dying*, in which she discusses the grieving process for people who learn they have a terminal illness. She suggests that grief is a five-stage process. Many parents of children with significant disabilities go through many of these stages of grief over the "loss" of the child they had thought they would have. A description of the Kubler-Ross Stages of Grief are listed in the box below, along with ways this process impacts parents of children with ELD.

These parents may go through a grieving process each time a developmental milestone fails to be met. Holidays and family get-togethers can be very trying as parents make comparisons with the children of friends and relatives. It is important to be aware that, in addition to the overwhelming demands of having a child with a significant disability, parents may also be trying to come to terms with their grief and sense of loss.

The Grieving Process
Adapted from *On Death and Dying* by Elizabeth Kubler-Ross

Stage 1: **Denial**	Initially, parents of a child diagnosed with a disability are in denial. They often mention all the things the child **can** do. Sometimes they comment on how another relative was "a little slow," and then was fine.
Stage 2: **Anger**	Often parents are angry and wonder *Why me?*
Stage 3: **Bargaining**	Parents try to bargain with God or a higher being. *If you just make our child okay, we promise we will do _____* or *If you just make our child okay, we promise we won't ever do _____.*
Stage 4: **Depression**	Parents often become depressed once they realize the diagnosis is correct.
Stage 5: **Acceptance**	In time, acceptance emerges for most parents. At this point, they can begin to enjoy the child they have and work hard to help him reach his full potential, whatever that may be.

Understanding Parents and the Internet

If information is power, then today's parents of children with disabilities are indeed empowered. From the Internet and the vast array of web sites devoted to special-needs children, parents can find a tremendous amount of information. Sometimes parents will judge professionals not by how good they are as therapists, but by how much they know.

I often have parents interview me to see if I am aware of the latest trends in treatment and what my results have been. They quiz me about my treatment approaches and my success with children with severe ELD. While some SLPs may find this attitude disconcerting, in some ways, it makes my job easier because I don't have to fill in a knowledge gap. I don't have to explain as much about the disability. Rather, I must explain my choice of treatment approaches. Sometimes I have to justify those choices. Savvy parents make me think and keep me on my toes. Once they are satisfied I know what I'm doing, these parents make excellent partners in therapy.

Siblings: The Little Heroes Among Us

I can never say enough about the courage of the siblings of children with disabilities. They are my wonderful little heroes. They are children who, like the entire family, must share the very adult responsibilities of caring for and supporting a child with disabilities. Their lives are often scheduled around therapy appointments and doctors' appointments.

Parents frequently try so hard to give the special-needs child the early stimulation and intervention needed that the siblings can feel forgotten. The siblings have mixed emotions. They want more attention from their parents, but sometimes feel guilty asking for it when they have no disabilities themselves.

Make the siblings feel important. Make them as much a part of the therapy process as possible. Let them know that what they do best, which is play with their sibling, is one of the most important therapeutic interventions possible. Be sure to convey all this information in "kid-friendly" language.

Group Therapy

Group therapy for children with ELD can have great or limited value, depending upon how it is structured. Typically, group therapy involves having children with communicative disorders participate together in language activities. There is certainly value to this type of interaction. Children learn to take turns, to listen to peers, and to attend to group activities. I think we should expand this notion of group therapy to include more typically-developing peers in an inclusive approach, being selective about which peers we include in the group and how we structure the group makeup.

When I do group therapy in preschools or elementary schools, I usually start by including one typical playmate. Remembering that expressive language is as much an emotional experience as it is anything else, I typically invite a playmate to "play" who, according to the teachers, has a natural attraction to the child with ELD and vice versa. These children are usually naturals for getting children with ELD to interact, engage, and talk. Later, I add additional therapy playmates as the child with ELD can handle it.

Other valuable sources of group interactions for the child with ELD are siblings, relatives, and neighborhood children. These children are often companions of the child with ELD, so natural carryover is virtually assured. Also, these children are already a big part of the child's life, so they are motivated to interact with the child. They choose to interact with the child as opposed to being scheduled to play with the child in a therapy setting; that's a profound difference from more traditional "group therapy." What better way to impact the life of the child with ELD than to improve the interactions with the child's closest peers?

Social-Skills Training

I vividly remember a little boy with whom I worked who was also participating in "social-skills training." The boy had very little interest in peers and few, if any, peer-interaction skills. His mom had asked me to watch a session to see if I had any thoughts.

The teacher arrived with her daughter, who was delightful. She went right over to the little boy, laughing and giggling. His face lit up.

The teacher told them to sit on the floor so they could begin the session. While the teacher read through her notes and pulled materials out of her bag, the little girl grew bored; she rolled back and stuck her feet up in the air. The little boy thought this was cool and did the same. She repeated it, and he imitated her. She changed her movement, and he followed her lead. This went on for several turns; they laughed hysterically, never taking their eyes off each other.

Then the teacher announced she was ready to begin their first activity, rolling a ball back and forth to each other. The little girl stared blankly at her mom. The little boy looked everywhere but where the "training" was going on.

The social-skills training session had ended before it began.

Challenging Behaviors Challenge Families

We must all be diligent in our attempts to manage challenging behavior. Parents must get as much assistance as possible. Severely-challenging behavior does all of the following:

- handicaps a child

- prevents learning

- limits opportunities for interactions with typical peers

- limits the expectations for positive outcomes

- makes life more difficult for the families of children with disabilities

Parents of children with severe disabilities must recognize challenging behavior and not be afraid to ask for help. Needing help managing the behavior of a child with severe disabilities is not a sign of failure or weakness. A generation ago, society felt that the behavior issues and learning difficulties of children with severe disabilities were best met by the state in residential "training" centers. Teams of specialists, including psychologists, speech therapists, occupational therapists, physical therapists, music therapists, recreational therapists, teachers, and behaviorists, were hired to meet the needs of severely-disabled children. Direct-care staff worked five-day weeks and eight-hour shifts; they also received ongoing training.

In a generation, attitudes have changed. We now know that isolating disabled children in large residential facilities was not in the best interests of the children. We realize that children ultimately do better being cared for in the community by their families. Efforts to move children out of institutions and back into communities began in earnest several years ago. Children newly-diagnosed with developmental disabilities remained with their families. Families, it was envisioned, would receive community support.

Unfortunately, in many instances, communities have not provided families with the support they need. We expect families with little or no training to do what teams of specialists with advanced degrees and years of experience in specially-designed facilities did a generation ago. Encourage parents to get help when they need it!

Language for a Lifetime

Language also occurs in the context of a lifetime. Language is an integral part of overall development. It is extremely important to see and understand the bigger picture of human development. In *Building Healthy Minds*, psychiatrist Greenspan suggests that we look at how all aspects of development function together in addition to identifying and assessing individual abilities, such as language development, social development, motor-skill development, sensory functioning, cognitive development, and visual-spatial skills.

"Although it is important to identify and assess specific aspects of development, for screening purposes, it is more useful to look at a child's overall 'functional' capacities. *How does a child simultaneously use his or her whole mental 'team' of specific abilities in a coordinated way to reach emotionally meaningful goals* is a new and useful way to think about development."

(1999, pg. 371)

Greenspan has identified six stages of development that are supported by the coordination of the capacities for language, motor coordination and sequencing, cognitive skills, and problem-solving skills:

Stage 1	The infant focuses on and attends to sights and sounds while remaining calm and regulated.
Stage 2	The infant engages in relationships. He "falls in love" with his parents.
Stage 3	The child learns to interact in a purposeful manner and becomes a two-way communicator.
Stage 4a	The child organizes chains of interaction for simple problem-solving and forms a sense of self.
Stage 4b	The child organizes chains of interaction for complex problem-solving and forms a sense of self.
Stage 5a	The child uses words and symbols to convey intentions or feelings.
Stage 5b	The child uses ideas, words, and symbols beyond expressing basic needs.
Stage 6a	The child creates logical bridges between ideas.
Stage 6b	The child creates logical bridges between three or more emotional ideas.

Greenspan suggests that an important feature of the coordinated development of capacities to move a child through developmental stages is a maturing sensory-processing system that allows the infant to organize and attend to sensory stimulation and later to enjoy the sensory feast of sights, sounds, tastes, textures, smells, and movement the world has to offer.

> ## Human Development Is More Than the Sum of Its Pieces

Know the School Curriculum

When a child goes to school, the language used to describe the child's development is encompassed in a curriculum. The *Brigance Diagnostic Inventory of Early Development* is a handy resource for expectations for preschool and early elementary grades. We SLPs and parents should be familiar with the curriculum for the child's school, and we should make sure that the language taught in therapy has relevance in the school setting. Furthermore, we must make sure the school the child attends supports the child's acquisition of truly **meaningful** language and communication skills.

Building Independence

For children with severe language disabilities, we must often provide many visual cues and supports for behavior regulation and skill acquisition. Photos, picture symbols, picture schedules, and picture sequences for multistep skills, such as hand washing, become an integral part of the child's life. We must be diligent in using these only for as long as a child needs them. If we continue to use the visual supports for longer than they are needed, then we are making the child more disabled, and we are limiting his ability to function in environments that are not rich in visual supports.

Moving Beyond Functional Communication

So much emphasis is placed on "functional communication" and "functional language" that sometimes we forget there is language and communication that a child can learn beyond what some consider functional communication. It's called **optimal communication**. Professionals have an obligation not to stop at simply functional communication. We must move a child as far as he can go. Don't be blindsided by a disability diagnosis or label.

I have a wonderful example of this. Several years ago, I treated a child who had what would now be diagnosed as autism spectrum disorder. When I first saw her, she was often engaged in isolated, perseverative play. She had little interest in contact with people. She had unusual responses to some sensory stimulation. At age three, she was essentially nonverbal. Her parents had covered all the bases in terms of approaches to facilitate language acquisition. She had behavioral-based treatment. She had interaction-based treatment in the preschool setting where I saw her. She also received therapy at a hospital outpatient clinic.

By the age of six, the little girl had made tremendous gains in therapy. The therapist at the outpatient clinic suggested that the little girl be discharged from therapy because she now had functional communication.

The mother was devastated. Yes, her daughter was functional, but she still was not functioning in the same way as the typical children in her school. She wondered if I would be discharging her daughter from therapy, too.

I indicated to the mother that her daughter had many things to learn and that, as long as she continued to show gains, I would see her in therapy. The little girl is steadily on a course for optimal functioning, and she is doing well. She's in a regular fourth grade. She has friends, baseball teams, soccer teams, and a part in the school play. She's gone well beyond "functional communication"!

Expanding Contexts—Building Bridges

As we envision children with ELD in the contexts of their lives, we must consider what we can do to expand those contexts. What can we do to make their communities more accessible to children with disabilities? *Accessibility* in this case does not mean physical accessibility. Rather, it means making communities more accessible to children by making communities more aware and more skilled at meeting the needs of children with disabilities. It means making the community part of the children's treatment teams for now and for the future. An example of this concept follows:

Gymnastics Classes

About seven years ago, my colleague and partner, Sandy, a sensory-integration-trained occupational therapist, asked what I thought about approaching the owner of a local gym, Jeff, to see if she and I could work with him to set up a sensory-integration-based, therapeutic gymnastics program for some of our special-needs preschoolers, particularly those with autism spectrum disorders.

We both had children who had attended gymnastic classes at Jeff's gym. I had two daughters who had been "on team" there. We were very excited about approaching Jeff, but we were realistic, too. Jeff was a former world-class gymnast who now trained junior Olympians and elite-level gymnasts. Can one go from training some of the most talented youngsters to some of the most challenging youngsters? That is asking a lot, but we approached him anyway. The worst that could happen is that he would say "No." To our surprise, we got a very enthusiastic "Yes!" Jeff commented that he had always wanted to do something like this, but wasn't sure how to go about it. So far, so good!

We set about the task of developing a program that addressed motor planning and sequencing, language processing, and sensory processing

(continued on next page)

as well as motor coordination. As the day of the first class approached, a sense of panic set in. Sandy and I knew what the first class would be like, and we had tried to prepare Jeff for it as well as we could. But how could we really prepare him for what we knew was to come?

As we expected, the first day was tough. Organized chaos. The environment was new and very stimulating. Some of the children were overwhelmed; some children wanted to explore everything. Some children loved to jump and swing; others were terrified. Some children loved to climb; others didn't want their feet to leave the ground. We were sure it was not like any other "first gym class" for Jeff. As realists, we were well aware that the first class might also be the last class, and that the first set of classes might also be the last. Boy, were we wrong!

After the first class, Jeff told us he loved it and began brainstorming with us as to how to make it ever better. The "'nastics" class, as the kids call it, is still going strong and has just started its sixth year. Some of our original kids have gone on to participate in regular recreational-gymnastics classes. Now Jeff and his staff feel more comfortable accepting children who present developmental challenges in their regular classes. In fact, just recently, Jeff did a national presentation on spotting techniques, including spotting techniques for special-needs children!

When Is It Too Late to Learn to Talk?

That is a difficult question to answer. I honestly don't know. Children who are motivated can do amazing things, as you'll see in the following stories.

Talking About Sadie

When Sadie was five, she was referred by the early interventionist who had worked with her family. Prior to meeting with Sadie, I met with her parents. They were clear in their hopes and aspirations for Sadie. They wanted her to talk. They had been told that if a child did not talk by age five, the chances that she would talk would be remote. What did I think? I told them that because she periodically produced words, although not imitatively or consistently, the prognosis was good. *(continued on next page)*

Sadie had received speech therapy from age two-and-a-half until age three. Her success at speech production had been minimal. Sadie reportedly had a few words, but would produce none of them when prompted. After listing what she had been heard to say, we began the task of getting consistent imitation.

The first few months were tough. Prompts for imitation for pleasure words or power words were usually met with severe tantrums. But in time, Sadie realized imitating words could be pretty rewarding. She was soon able to imitate two words consistently, one pleasure word (*whee*) and one power word (*open*). Shortly thereafter, she was able to alternate between these two words. Within a few months, she was able to produce an approximation for almost any word prompted for imitation. Spontaneous speech emerged as well. She loved to fill the lines to songs and finger plays. Her early favorite, hands down, was Winnie the "Pooh"!

Jack's Story

Jack was an eight-year-old with Down syndrome. "I want him to talk," said Jack's dad. "Can you teach him to talk?"

I said I didn't know. I typically started with children much younger than eight, but I would try.

Jim could produce a few nonsense syllables and nothing more. I wasn't sure how far he could go, but I would certainly give it some time before saying he would never be able to speak.

I decided to try to teach Jack to talk the same way I would teach a younger child. To my surprise, Jack could imitate sounds. I had presented him with the Picture Sound Stimulus Cards I often use, and he loved them. We quickly turned his sounds into some very powerful and pleasurable word approximations. "Hi, Mom" was one of the first things he learned to say, and he loved it. Over the next twelve months, Jim acquired many more words and word approximations. Still, in the back of my mind, I wondered if he was motivated to use them.

(continued on next page)

181

Then I got the answer to my question. One day when we were walking back to his classroom, Jack saw a lady wearing a T-shirt with a schoolbus on it. He loved schoolbuses. He was driven to school by his mom, so he did not have a chance to ride the bus. He ran up to the lady and asked, "That (s)chool bu(s)?"

She looked down at him and smiled. "Yes, you are right," she said. "It is a schoolbus." He was so excited to be understood and hold a "real conversation."

Speaking of Nadene

Nadene was referred to me at the age of 12. She had a diagnosis of mild CP and autism, and she was nonverbal. I had assumed that her referral was for work on developing an augmentative communication system.

As I began my discussion with Nadene's mom, I mentioned several courses of action we could take. There were a number of really wonderful devices available. Mom listened patiently. Then she asked, "But can you teach her to talk?" I paused and fumbled for a response. How could I say in a kind way that she was too old?

Before I could answer, Nadene's mom said, "No one has ever really tried to teach her to talk. Please try before we give up on it." I agreed.

Later, Nadene's mom said, "Just to hear my daughter say 'Hi, Mom' and 'Hi, Dad' has made all the difference in our lives. It is wonderful to hear her say *no* instead of screaming when she doesn't want something."

Nadene has a renewed interest in people and in learning. She is feeling the power and pleasure of spoken language. Granted, speech is not Nadene's only mode of communication, but she has learned to say many words and is beginning to produce two-word combinations. Learning to speak has been a struggle for Nadene, but a struggle worth *every* ounce of effort for this hard-working young lady.

Glossary of Terms

apraxia — A disorder characterized by difficulty with voluntary sequenced movement in the absence of weakness or paralysis

attribute — A description of a feature of something, such as its size, shape, color, texture, or function

carrier phrase — A common phrase that is used repeatedly as information is put into practice sentences. For example, *I see the ___*.

criterion-referenced test — An assessment in which the performance of an individual is measured against a standard or criterion rather than against others taking the same test

echolalia — Exact repetition of an utterance; may be immediate or delayed

entity — Any word used as a noun

literacy — Of or relating to reading and writing

locative — An adverb that tells information about place, such as *here, there*, or *on*

norm-referenced test — An assessment in which an individual's performance is evaluated in relation to the performance of others in the norm group

percentile rank — Indicates the percentage of individuals tested who have scored equal to or lower than a specific score. For example, a percentile rank of 70 means that 70% of the individuals who took the test scored the same score or lower.

phoneme — The shortest unit of sound in a language that is recognized as different from other sounds in that language, such as /m/ as in *mom*

phonology — The study of speech sounds, patterns, and rules to create words for a given language

pragmatics — The use of language in social contexts for communicative purposes

recurrence — An action or object that recurs after an interval. Children request recurrence by saying "more" as in *more ball* and *more tickle*.

referent — The person or object that a word indicates or refers to

Glossary of Terms, *continued*

standard score

The results when a raw score is transformed into a standard form based on the normal distribution curve. For many instruments, the mean is 100, one standard deviation below the mean is 85, and one standard deviation above the mean is 115. In a normal distribution, approximately $2/3$ of the scores fall between 85 and 115.

standard deviation

The amount of the deviation of a score from the mean score for the distribution. In the normal population, approximately $2/3$ of the scores fall within the limits of one standard deviation above and one standard deviation below the mean score.

standardized test

A test that has undergone standardization procedures so that an individual's performance can be compared to other individuals of the same chronological age. Typically, standardized tests have very specific test directions, data on the sample on which the norms are based, and reliability and validity data.

norm group

The representative group of individuals whose test scores are used to establish a reference set of norms for a standardized test score. It is important that the individual to be tested fit the normative population description for a given standardized test.

reliability

The consistency with which a test measures what it is designed to measure

validity

The extent to which a test measures what it purports to measure

Resources

Organizations

For information about preschools and developmentally-appropriate preschool activities, contact:

National Association for the Education of Young Children
1509 16th Street N.W.
Washington, D.C. 20036
Phone: 202-232-8777
               800-424-2460
FAX: 202-328-1846

For information about speech and language disorders, contact:

American Speech-Language-Hearing Association
10801 Rockville Pike
Rockville, MD 20852
Phone: 301-897-5700
FAX: 301-571-0457
Web: www.asha.org
E-mail: irc@asha.org

For information about a variety of subjects related to children with language and learning disabilities, contact:

The Unicorn Children's Foundation
5401 N.W. Broken Sound Boulevard
Boca Raton, FL 33487
Phone: 888-782-8321
     561-989-1140
Web: www.saveachild.com
E-mail: Unicorn@SaveaChild.com

For information about sensorimotor processing and sensory integrative dysfunction, contact:

Sensory Integration International
P.O. Box 9013
1602 Cabrillo Avenue
Torrance, CA 90501
Phone: 310-320-9986
FAX: 310-320-9934
Web: www.earthlink.net/ (Search for *sensoryint.*)
E-mail: sensoryint@earthlink.net

Resources, *continued*

For information about strategies to manage behavior and to teach skills, contact:

The Association of Behavior Analysis
213 West Hall
Western Michigan University
1201 Oliver Street
Kalamazoo, MI 49008-4052
Phone: 616-387-8341
FAX: 616-387-8354
E-mail: 76236.1312@compuserve.com

Books and Materials

LinguiSystems is a great source for photo vocabulary cards, auditory processing and listening materials, preschool activities, and sequenced picture stories.

LinguiSystems, Inc.
3100 4th Avenue
East Moline, IL 61244-9700
Phone: 800-776-4332
FAX: 800-577-4555
Web: www.linguisystems.com
E-mail: service@linguisystems.com

Imaginart has a wonderful catalog entitled *Resources for Children with Autism*. The photo cards, games, and sequencing activities are appropriate for children with all types of ELD.

Imaginart
307 Arizona Street
Bisbee, AZ 85603
Phone: 800-828-1376
FAX: 800-737-1376

DK (Dorling Kindersley) Publishers' books appeal to children because of their high-quality color photography. See especially their wonderfully appealing and imaginative "First Steps to Reading Series."

DK Publishing, Inc.
95 Madison Avenue
New York, NY 10016
Phone: 212-213-4800
FAX: 212-213-5240
Web: www.dk.com

Resources, *continued*

Golden Books, Inc., produces the excellent *Road to Reading* series:

> Golden Books, Inc.
> 10101 Science Drive
> Sturtevant, WI 53177
> Phone: 800-236-7123

Scholastic, Inc., produces the *Hello Reader!* series, among others:

> Scholastic, Inc.
> 555 Broadway
> New York, NY 10012
> Phone: 800-724-6527
> Web: www.scholastic.com

Troll Learn and Play has products associated with popular commercial characters, including stickers, stamps, books, and puzzles. They also carry crafts materials and props and costumes for dress-up play:

> Troll Learn and Play
> 1950 Waldorf N.W.
> Grand Rapids, MI 49550-7100
> Phone: 800-247-6106
> FAX: 800-451-0812

Related Programs

Lindamood-Bell programs are designed to develop the sensory-cognitive processes that underlie reading, spelling, math, visual-motor skills, language comprehension, and critical thinking:

> Lindamood-Bell Learning Processes
> Gander Educational Publishing
> 412 Higuerra Street, Suite 200
> San Luis Obispo, CA 93401
> Phone: 800-233-1819

Scientific Learning Corporation materials, including Fast ForWord, are designed to develop skills critical for listening, thinking, and reading:

> Scientific Learning Corporation
> 1995 University Avenue, Suite 400
> Berkeley, CA 94704
> Phone: 888-665-9707
> FAX: 510-665-1279

References

Ayres, A. J. *Sensory Integration and the Child.* Los Angeles, CA: Western Psychological Services, 1979.

Brigance, A. *Brigance Diagnostic Inventory of Early Development: Birth to Seven Years.* Revised. North Billerica, MA: Curriculum Associates, Inc., 1991.

Gillette, Y. and MacDonald, J. D. *Eco Resources.* San Antonio, TX: Special Press, Inc., 1989.

Greenspan, S. I., and Lewis, N. B. (contributor). *Building Healthy Minds.* Cambridge, MA: Perseus Books, 1999.

Greenspan, S. I. and Weider, S. *The Child with Special Needs.* Reading, MA: Addison-Wesley, 1998.

Hedge, M. N. *Treatment Procedures in Communicative Disorders.* 3rd Edition. Austin, TX: Pro-Ed, 1998.

Kranowitz, C. S. *The Out-of-Sync Child: Recognizing and Coping with Sensory Integration Dysfunction.* New York, NY: The Berkley Publishing Group, 1998.

Kubler-Ross, E. *On Death and Dying.* New York, NY: Simon and Schuster, 1997.

Locke, J. L. *The Child's Path to Spoken Language.* Cambridge, MA: Harvard University Press, 1993.

Lovaas, O. I. *The Me Book.* Baltimore, MD: University Park Press, 1981.

Maurice, C., Green, G., and Luce, S., eds. *Behavioral Intervention for Young Children with Autism: A Manual for Parents and Professionals.* Austin, TX: Pro-Ed, 1996.

Manolson, A. *It Takes Two to Talk: A Parent's Guide to Helping Children Communicate.* Available from the Hanen Centre, Suite 3-390, 252 Bloor St., West Toronto, ON, M5S 1V5, 1996.

National Institute on Deafness and Other Communication Disorders. *National Strategic Research Plan for Language and Language Impairments, Balance and Balance Disorders, and Voice and Voice Disorders.* NIT Publication No. 97-3217. Bethesda, MD: 1995.

Nelson, N. W. *Childhood Language Disorders in Context: Infancy Through Adolescence.* 2nd Edition. Boston, MA: Allyn and Bacon, 1998.

Tomblin, J. B., Smith, E., and Zhang, X. "Prevalence of Specific Language Impairment in Kindergarten Children." *Journal of Speech, Language, Hearing Research,* Vol. 40, 1997.

Warren, S. F. and Reichle, J. *Causes and Effects in Communication and Language Intervention.* Vol. 1. Baltimore, MD: Paul H. Brooks Publishing Co., 1992.